The Other Side of the Mountain

Gerald O'Mahony

SECOND EDITION

Fisher Miller
PUBLISHING

First published 1989 by Geoffrey Chapman, an imprint of Cassell Publishers Ltd, Artillery House, Artillery Row, London, SW1P 1RT

This edition published 1998 by Fisher Miller Publishing, Wits End, 11 Ramsholt Close, North Waltham, Basingstoke, Hants, RG25 2DG United Kingdom

Printed by Redwood Books

ISBN 1-899077-05-7

A catalogue record for this book is available from the British Library

The moral right of Gerald O'Mahony to be identified as the author of this work has been asserted.

Acknowledgements

Sincere thanks to Mary Parkinson for sorting out and typing most of the script.

Scripture quotations are taken from the Jerusalem Bible, published and copyright 1966, 1967, 1968 by Darton, Longman and Todd Ltd and Doubleday, a division of Bantam, Doubleday, Dell Publishing Group, Inc. Reprinted by permission.

Cover photograph courtesy the author.

Contents

Preface to the new updated edition

It is now ten years since I wrote the first edition of this book. Two years after that I had found a willing publisher; now eight years after *that*, all the copies have been sold, and whereas I can see a continuing demand for the book, the original publishers feel they cannot justify a reprint. So with a lot of help from friends, relations and benefactors, and with the blessing of the original publishers Geoffrey Chapman/Cassell plc, here is a new edition brought out by Fisher Miller Publishing. While we were about it, the time seemed ripe for an update of the story, to cover the next ten years, from 1987 to 1997. This is included at the end of the story, where it belongs.

Gerald O'Mahony
Loyola Hall Spirituality Centre
August 1997

Introduction

THE SEARCH FOR GOD

This is the story of one man's search for God. 'Search, and you will find', said Jesus. On my journey, which please God is far from over yet, I have been greatly helped by the story of other people's lives, particularly the story of their inner lives, hidden with God. So I wish to tell my own story, in my own way, not as an autobiography but rather as the story of what thoughts about God formed the basis of my life at different stages of my life, in the hope that some others may be helped and encouraged by reading it.

For the search after God, or the climbing of the Rock, or the journey into God, is a matter of getting to know him better. We each have our notion of who God is and what God is like, we act on it, and discover we were partly right and partly wrong. He is both more mysterious and more lovable than we thought. So we move to a new understanding of God, and begin to act as if that were the whole truth — until he shows a little more of himself, and we move forward yet again. In all I can trace seven different ways of looking at God in my own life so far, and these will form the basis of the seven chapters of this book.

You will discover that each chapter has the same underlying structure. At the beginning of each chapter there is a section with a short account of how I came one day to climb the Mediterranean Steps in Gibraltar. What have these instalments of another tale to do with my life-story? The climb itself, up the eastern or Mediterranean side of the Rock of Gibraltar, is very simple, a pleasant afternoon's walk rather than any feat of mountaineering; but in reflecting on it afterwards, it just seemed to fall neatly into seven stages illustrating the seven ways of looking at God that I wished to write about.

The second section of each chapter is the telling of my life-story, or more exactly, the story of the seven ways of understanding the God who forms the basis of my life-story.

Following the second main section of each chapter, where I describe the events and experiences, both inward and outward, of each stage of my journey, I have placed a third section of Scriptural passages. There are some passages of Scripture which remind us strongly, whenever we read them, of a particular time in our own lives. Some are important to us at the time, others we recognize only in retrospect as applying to ourselves. Between the various stages of my life and those in most other people's lives there are almost bound to be some similarities. Although we each have our own mountain to climb, there will always be similarities between one mountain and another. And if certain passages of the Bible have, for instance, helped me make sense of my early years, up to the time I left school and joined the Jesuits, they may appeal to others as well when they reflect on their childhood and youth. So you will find each chapter has a third section, in which I mention those Bible passages which seem to me to belong especially with that particular period of my life.

All that I describe about my own life may appear to be very 'religious', but I am convinced that the underlying experiences are shared by much of the human race. So after the Scripture section in each chapter I end with a fourth, making a few comparisons between my life and the lives of lay people, and suggesting (as far as possible without the use of Bible passages) where the common ground may lie, even if it is not immediately obvious. Then the words of Scripture which make sense of that part of life for me may perhaps be found to shed light and help on many other people's lives besides mine.

One thought about God has stayed with me all through my life. I have always wanted to be a good servant of God. So rather than attempt to describe my thoughts about God and how they changed with the years, I have preferred to follow the fortunes of that one idea, 'servant of God', in the ups and downs of my own life. The title of being God's servant is something common to all Christians, and indeed all people of good will, so any reader will, I hope, feel at home when I write mainly about serving God. But I am aware that while 'servant' is a word which speaks volumes to me, to a fellow Christian it may be just one word among many.

I am aware, too, that we do not all experience the key events of our lives in the same order. Some people, for instance, have to go through suffering much earlier in their lives than I did; some find themselves unable to decide until much later than I what to do with their lives; others again feel themselves unwanted, because what they would like to do proves to be impossible. So all I plan to do is simply to take the pattern of my own life as a tentative model. Not just I but everyone is called to service, and the ideal of service is able to embrace both sickness and disappointment, since a servant may be sick or may be locked up, may fail or be a latecomer, without ceasing to be a good servant. In the end God does not so much reward our performance as fulfil our desires.

I
First Sight

1·THE PATH

One day several years ago on a visit to Gibraltar I was being given a tour of the Rock. One place we stopped at was near the southern end, where a signpost pointed along a footpath to the Mediterranean Steps. These steps, we were told, were the only way of climbing up the extremely steep eastern side of the Rock, starting from where we stood and ending on the ridge at the summit about a thousand feet above. We were curious, and went to have a closer look, I and the friend I was with, and the Gibraltarian friend who was showing us round. The path to begin with was dusty but very pleasant, along level ground with some trees to offer shade from the Mediterranean heat. There was a profusion of wild flowers, and always the view of the sea and of Europa Point at the southern tip of the Rock to our right. To our left the bulk of the Rock towered.

We had been toying with the idea of climbing the Steps when we came to them, even of climbing to the top. But when we came to the first of the steps, they led down, not up. My English friend and I were surprised, though our friend who was guiding us remembered that this would be the case: the steps go down first, then up. Well, the afternoon felt hotter and there were no trees by this time. If we went on, intending to reach the top, it would mean going down first, every step down adding to the height to be climbed afterwards. Even if we just went on a little way to investigate, we would have to climb back up again to where we now were. So we decided enough was enough, and went back to the road and the car. But I was intrigued by what I had seen, and promised myself, if the chance should occur again, to climb those Mediterranean Steps to the top.

1

2·AN EARLY CALL

Whether we know it or not, we all have a journey into God, and it starts at the very beginning of our lives. I have for instance known a little girl who was given a nurse's uniform at the age of seven and went round curing everyone who would play the game: she has since become a highly qualified nurse. Among boys near my own age there was one who was forever making model aeroplanes, planes that flew: he became an airline pilot. Another, who enjoyed making huts of stone and wood for his friends to use as dens, grew up to be an architect. There is something inside all of us which is special to ourselves alone, and which we can usually see, when we look back, to be something that started when we were very young. If our first ambition turns out to be beyond our reach or no longer within our reach, we turn to something similar within our reach. Someone who wanted to be a doctor may find even greater happiness working in some other way for healing within the community. Those who are unemployed may find satisfaction in voluntary work, or a hobby, or at any rate in something they do well.

Looking back on my own life, I would say that the first signs of what I now know is my vocation — to be a servant of God — came to me some time in 1940 about a year after the outbreak of the Second World War, when I was six years old. My picture of God from as early as I can remember had been of someone very friendly. I can recall making a deal with him early on, before the war, that in heaven just the two of us (consciously or unconsciously I was speaking to the Father) would go hand in hand to every interesting place in the universe, especially the jungles and the South Sea islands, and he would show me everything and how he made it. There would be no hurry and we could take as long as we felt like taking; in this life there did not seem to be time enough for such world-gazing. I still smile when I find myself watching one of the breathtaking wild-life documentaries in full colour on the television, and just for a half-hour or so I am taken on very much the kind of tour I had in mind as a little boy. Then when the war broke out, what with the news on the radio, photographs and maps in the papers, and our parents' answers

2

to our questions, even young children could get a sense of what was going on. The whole world was obviously in a mess; to me with my Catholic upbringing it seemed clear that God (and here I suppose I had Jesus in mind) was in charge of putting the world to rights again and healing everyone, and that he needed help from volunteers, since he works through people. At the time I rather fancied becoming a sailor, having already gone through wanting to be a dustbin man, an engine driver and a fireman. With this new desire to help God I decided to be a chaplain in the Royal Navy, which I thought was a rather neat compromise.

But whereas the yearning to be a sailor soon took less and less room in my heart, the decision to be a priest stayed on, and never afterwards left me. So far as I remember, I never breathed a word about it to anyone, even at home, between the ages of seven and seventeen. To begin with, this was because I did not want to be thought a cissy, and later, in adolescence, I probably kept quiet because I did not want the girls I knew to find out and treat me as a stranger. Along with the friendly picture of God I enjoyed in childhood had come in adolescence a desire and determination to be 'friend of all the world' like Rudyard Kipling's Kim, and not even the deep desire to be a priest was going to make me hide away from the girls who came into my young life. I would be friends with them as with everyone. But I did keep a distance in the sense that I never consciously followed up any friendship with a girl if it could have become really close. It seemed unfair to invite any girl to risk falling in love with me when I would then have to leave her. Marriage for me was a beautiful thing for which there just was no time in this life, for me at any rate, because of the urgency of Jesus' call for help. He would sort something out in heaven.

To go back to the beginning: school lessons soon began to drive a wedge between God and me. I can remember one lesson most vividly; I was six at the time. The teacher told us that for every good deed we did in this life God in heaven would take one jewel-encrusted golden brick and put it towards the building of our heavenly mansion, our own personal house and home-to-be. Lots of good deeds down here would mean lots of golden bricks up there, and a lovely big house in heaven to go to when we died. I am pretty sure she also went on to state the obvious corollary, that if we did bad deeds or naughty things, for every bad deed God would shake his head sadly and remove one golden brick from our house, giving it perhaps to someone more deserving. I certainly took in the message, that if in the end my bad deeds were more than my good ones, I would end up with no mansion at all, no home in heaven, no place in God's heart, nothing but hell. Besides which, all of us children were thus placed in competition with each other and the rest of the world. Religion became just like school writ large, with top-of-the-class at one end of the scales and expulsion at the other. Such doctrine is of course heresy, the Pelagian heresy that human beings can achieve salvation through their own efforts, and quite simply poisonous. We do not earn our place in heaven, we need not fight to gain our own place in our Father's heart. But as a child in that class I swallowed the poisoned apple, and it was like the fall from the garden of Eden in my small life.

The vocation, however, to be a servant of God, and the belief in God's love, somehow survived not only the episode of the golden bricks but also the hair-raising teaching about mortal sin and the Sacrament of Penance which followed. Mortal sin was everywhere, hell an almost daily companion, and the Sacrament of Penance for me created at least as many problems as it solved. Those were rough times for sensitive children, to say nothing of sensitive adults. From my first Confession at the age of six till the age of twenty-four I was desperately scrupulous. Yet there was something deeper within me which made me sure I was doing the right thing when in 1952, at the age of eighteen, I joined the Jesuits to train as a priest. I wonder whether we would still have invented fears about not deserving heaven, and still have created scruples within ourselves, if as children we had been told the truth about God's love and forgiveness? I have a strong feeling that human beings, no matter how well taught, inevitably go through a phase of loving God, then of losing confidence in his love, then of finding him again at a deeper level. The experience seems to me rather like that of the mountaineer: as he approaches the mountain to climb it, he can see the summit clearly from a good distance away but as he reaches the foothills and sets up his base camp, he cannot see the summit any more, because the shoulders of the mountain get in the way. This blindness can be quite dispiriting. Only when he gets a good deal higher can he see the top again, and the sight of the summit gives him added strength. Our childhood teaching made us small climbers doubt at times whether the top of our mountain — a loving

4

God — existed any more; some other miserable target seemed to block our vision. Surely religious education should counteract our instinctive fears rather than reinforce them.

How I came to be a Jesuit priest rather than any other kind was like this: the Roman Catholic secondary school I was at was run by Jesuits, and we used to have an annual school retreat. The retreat director in the year I was sixteen was Father Joseph Christie, SJ, and in one talk he ran through a whole list of possible vocations, both lay and religious, giving a thumbnail sketch of each. When he came to the Jesuit vocation, he said Jesuits were God's odd-job men: a Jesuit might find himself in a home parish, in a school at home or abroad teaching, as a missioner living in some remote part of Asia or Africa, working in the Vatican Observatory as an astronomer, doing anything anywhere in the world, depending on where the need was. To the usual three monastic vows of poverty, chastity and obedience, St Ignatius Loyola, who founded the Jesuit order, the Society of Jesus, in 1540, had added a fourth: Jesuits must be ready at a moment's notice to undertake any mission, whatsoever and wherever it might be, even at risk of their lives. That was enough for me. From then on, I not only had the mountain to climb but I had a path which I knew would suit me. To be a priest was only secondary after that. I would have been just as content if the Jesuit superiors had asked me to live among them as a Brother instead of as a priest. I am a companion of Jesus first, a priest only because my superiors thought that best.

Such, then, is a summary of the first stage of my journey into God, my first eighteen years. Something stirred me as if from the far end of my life; the mountain-top called me. As I came closer I lost clear sight of the top but knew it was still there; I found a path; but I had to wait awhile before starting on the journey. My mother noticed that in the last summer holidays before I went off to join the Jesuits, I was a lot lazier and less prayerful than usual. She wondered how I would stand the pace in the novitiate, the probationary period of training and testing for those wishing to enter a religious order, before taking their vows.

Of all the names people call me when I have exasperated them, 'useless' is the one that hurts me most. Usually the adjective has to do with my being impractical, less than a Robinson Crusoe for enterprise. I am sure the name 'useless' hurts so much because it describes the exact opposite of what I know myself called to be, namely a servant. So I have over the years had to learn two special truths, for my own peace of mind. The first is, that I am called not to be every Jesuit, just this Jesuit, not every servant, but this one servant. Between us all on this earth, we have enough skills; separately we do not amount to much, but we each contribute the particular skills we have. The second truth is this: 'servant' describes my constant target, my desire and not my performance. That is what I want to be, a good servant of God.

3·'MY CHOSEN ONE . . . MY SERVANT'

To begin at the beginning, there are two quotations from the prophet Isaiah that take me back to my birth, to before my birth, to before my conception. I did not know these quotations until well on into my adult life, when as a student for the priesthood I first heard about the four songs of the Servant of Yahweh (God) to be found in the second part of Isaiah. In lectures we were shown how Jesus in the gospels understood his life and his death in the light of these four songs; we were shown too that every Christian is called to be a servant of God such as those songs describe, insofar as every Christian is called to be 'another Christ'. Given my own ambition to be a servant of God, I quickly recognized myself in the Servant Songs as if in a mirror, and made them my own. But then if I am (or anybody is) the servant of God, it follows that God must have chosen me, chosen us, before we were born. My name, my nature, as servant of God was chosen by God before I was born.

Here are the two quotations. In the first Servant Song Yahweh (God) speaks:

> Here is my servant whom I uphold,
> my chosen one in whom my soul delights (Isaiah 42:1).

And in the second Song the Servant says:

> Yahweh called me before I was born,
> from my mother's womb he pronounced my name . . .
> . . . He said to me, 'You are my servant' (Isaiah 49:1, 3).

6

If I am called to be another Christ, then these prophecies are spoken about all his followers, about me as well as about Jesus, about him first but about me afterwards. So I am a servant of God; he upholds me; I too am his chosen one. He had chosen me already when I was in my mother's womb. Lest we think such words too marvellous to be true of ourselves, St Paul tells us in one of his own songs that God chose us in Christ before ever the world was made (cf. Ephesians 1:4). God called me his servant before anyone on earth thought of me. In the story of the coming into the world of both Jesus and St John the Baptist his forerunner, St Luke tells how their names were chosen by God before they were conceived. 'You must name him Jesus' Mary was told, and 'You must name him John' was told to Zechariah (Luke 1:13, 31). Some famous leaders of past centuries, like Samuel the judge and prophet and Samson the judge, had been chosen by God before they were conceived, yet for all their greatness they called themselves God's servants (cf. 1 Samuel 3:9; Judges 15:18). Since the babies were too tiny to do their own rejoicing at being chosen, Hannah his mother sang a song for Samuel (1 Samuel 2), Zechariah sang for John, and Mary for Jesus still in her womb (Luke 1).

Although I now see myself as in a mirror in those two short quotations from Isaiah (and moreover the mirror is there for anyone else to look into as well), yet early on, as a child and as a schoolboy, I did not think of myself as chosen in that way, nor would I even have called myself 'servant' before God. All I had was a general desire to be useful and helpful, and a particular desire to go and help God. What form the help might take I had no idea: God would tell me that when I got there, when I joined the Jesuits as it turned out. Except in a few important particulars, I have always been a lieutenant by nature rather than a leader of men. To be a servant has always seemed to me to be a laudable ambition. My early warm feelings towards the word 'servant' probably came as much out of stories from the Arabian Nights and various fairy tales as from any religious source. In the story of Cinderella I identified far more with Buttons the servant than with the prince. Only recently did it occur to me that of course one who is called to be a servant will from a very early age enjoy stories about grand viziers, resourceful servants, speedy messengers and faithful sheepdogs.

'In love you created us.' I was from the beginning very happy to believe that God created us in love. I loved so many things — the first sight of the sea, the scent of daphne beside our front door, the scent of lily-of-the-valley beside our front gate, days out climbing hills with the family, specks of dust floating in sunbeams, the smell of bacon and eggs, the sight of the planet Venus seen through a neighbour's telescope, the warm glow of the gasfire (in the room I shared with my brother) when I was getting better from some sickness. A loving father and mother, sister and brother, what more could anyone ask for? To be at the service of God seemed perfectly natural to me in my very early years, just as it was natural to the sun, the moon and the stars, the earth and all its plants and animals. 'Yahweh . . . you use the winds as messengers and fiery flames as servants' (Psalm 104:4); 'creation is maintained by your rulings, since all things are your servants' (Psalm 119:91). If I could have understood the words, I would have felt at home with prayers like 'My Strength, I play for you, my citadel is God himself, the God who loves me' (Psalm 59:17), or 'rest in God, my safety, my glory, the rock of my strength' (Psalm 62:7). This of course was before well-meaning but misguided teachers had put into my mind that God might send me to hell for ever some day, and that he was even now weighing my good deeds against the bad.

My actual vocation is brought to my mind most vividly by the story of Abraham's call, rather than by any other call described in the Bible. He is 'servant of Yahweh', the first in the Bible story to call himself 'your servant' in speaking to Yahweh, the God we now know as our Father (Genesis 18:3, 5). He is called to a far country which he does not yet know (Genesis 12), and enormous consequences rest on that simple call — a whole race of people and two world religions. The call of Abraham is the beginning of the story of a people in its dealings with God. My own call, to go and help God in whatever part of the world he might want me, occurred, as I have said, when I was six years old. And the consequences, though not earthshaking, are nonetheless far beyond anything I imagined when I was called. My call was so gentle that I did not know it had happened until months afterwards, at the point where I stopped talking about being a naval chaplain and began to make non-committal answers if people asked me what I was going to be when I grew up.

Although for some mysterious reason our Scripture lessons in primary school ran only from the creation story as far as the Ten Commandments, and then skipped on a thousand years and more to the New Testament, our early lessons did as a result include the story of Abraham. But it never occurred to me then to look into his call and see my own. Abraham seemed to hear voices and see visions, whereas I had simply found my mind made up. A call which did impress me was that of the young boy Samuel, disturbed in his sleep three times and then a fourth time by God. Each of the first three times Samuel ran to old Eli to ask him what he wanted. At last Eli recognized that it was God who was calling Samuel; he told the boy if the call came again to get up and say 'Speak, Yahweh, your servant is listening' (cf. 1 Samuel 3:1–18). That was one further passage from the Old Testament which did come into our Scripture programme. I liked and remembered the story, but again did not at the time see any connection between Samuel's vocation and my own.

As often as not, the servant of God is also called to be a prophet, a speaker for God. Jesus himself is both Servant and Prophet. In Jesus' story of the wicked husbandmen, the prophets of the Old Testament figure as servants, servants of the owner of the vineyard, sent to relay the owner's requests (cf. Mark 12:2). Already in the Old Testament God is often shown referring to 'my servants the prophets' (e.g. Kings 21:10). In a general way, as my schooldays went by, I was aware that as a servant of God I would be called upon to take God's message to people I did not know, even though at the time I did not see any urgency in the message itself. I did not see myself as called to be a minister of the word, a servant of the word (cf. Luke 1:2). I was simply at the service of God, and he would tell me what to say when the time of sending out came. 'Servant of the Church' (Colossians 1:25) was a title that would have made sense to me at this time, since the Church was the structure out of which my orders would come, just as the Church had been, through my church-going family, the source of my inspiration. I now know that 'I am sent by God' is only the other side of the coin from 'I am called by God'; as a young person I knew myself called, but was still waiting to be sent.

Service was also connected in my mind with the priesthood (Luke 1:8, 23). A priest would be at the service of the Church and of the whole world, as I could see verified in the priests I

9

met at home and at school and elsewhere. Jesus wanted helpers, part-time or full-time, and there were not enough of them to go round. The harvest was plentiful, but the labourers were few (cf. Matthew 9:37). Just as Jesus appealed to Peter and James and John and Andrew and Matthew to follow him, so I wanted to leave everything and follow him (cf. Mark 1:16–20; Matthew 9:9). As the time came closer for going away from home I was already aware that following Jesus might entail a certain rugged simplicity: messengers called by God to prepare the way are not expected to dress in fine clothes and live in palaces (cf. Luke 7:24–27). Nor do they put their own safety or convenience first: Jesus planned to have a quiet time with his apostles, but when the crowds in their thousands got to the quiet place first, he did not take the boat and the apostles elsewhere: he stepped ashore and cared for the hungry people (cf. Mark 6:30–44). Jesus' story of the Good Samaritan shows us his ideal for himself as well as for us, a man who does not think of his position or status in life, but at no little risk to himself has compassion on a wounded traveller, whom he heals and feeds and restores to health (cf. Luke 10:29–37). I did not really see danger ahead for myself in the vocation to the priesthood: the world war was over; not many of the places a priest might be sent to at that time carried a risk to life from violence. However, I do not think I would have been completely surprised if some seer had told me that before I was fifty years old we would have lost six of our fellow Jesuits from this country by violent deaths, four of them in Zimbabwe and two in Guyana. Missionaries living abroad have always been subject to danger, and missionaries at home have always been subject to hostility and persecution. To my young eyes, the cross in one form or another seemed to be the lot of all human beings, and especially of anyone who set out to try and help fellow travellers in trouble. To a young volunteer the spice of danger can even be part of the attraction.

Jesus on the way to Jerusalem in his last months was still having to teach his disciples the way of humility. 'What were you arguing about on the road?' he asked them, knowing very well they had been discussing which of them was the greatest (cf. Mark 9:33–37). If the apostles after two years or more in the company of Jesus were still arguing about such a thing, small wonder that I was rather arrogant as a child and as a young man, inclined to think I had all the answers to everything and nobody else knew a thing. A few months in the school debating society and I fancied myself as a future Prime Minister. Setting out on a life of service in the Jesuits, I immediately wanted it to be the greatest service, not for Jesus' sake but for mine. I was not altogether unlike the Pharisee, willing to travel over land and sea to make a single convert, only to make that convert twice as worried about weighing good deeds against bad and keeping the law as I was (cf. Matthew 23:15).

Even though I have been quoting passages from the New Testament as shedding light for me on my early life, yet in a certain sense my life was still governed by the Old Testament. After a happy garden-of-Eden beginning at home, I was taught at school all about the Ten Commandments and the Sacrament of Penance in such a way as to make life seem like a race to keep ahead of God's pursuing anger. We children were indeed introduced to Jesus by our teachers, and we learnt a lot about Jesus from them as loving people, but not from their lessons. With the lessons, we were still in the land of 'If you keep the Ten Commandments, God will love you, but not otherwise', and 'If you come back and make a good confession, God will love you, but not otherwise'. God's love was conditional. I suppose the apostles themselves were still in the world of the old covenant, until the new covenant had been established by Jesus in his own blood (cf. Luke 22:20).

One last impression from these years is worth mentioning, because it will appear later in another form. When I thought about Jesus, pictured Jesus or prayed to him at this time, he was always apart from me. He was there, I was here; he was walking, I was following.

4·TO EACH OF US SOMETHING UNIQUE

Not some, but all of us were chosen by God before the world was made. God has no favourites, as both St Peter and St Paul remind us, so if he chooses one he chooses all. The Chosen People were not so much the only ones chosen, as the first to see we are all chosen. Just as God knows each one of the countless stars by its own name, so he has known each one of us by name since before we were conceived. And coming into the world we found ourselves called, along with the whole human race, to be stewards of creation. Stewardship is a vocation; marriage too, and the raising of a family has been part of most people's vocation from the beginning of time: a man and woman together, called to be stewards of the earth. Yet very few people would be able to remember that moment at which they first perhaps felt responsible for the earth, or for one another, or first knew they wanted to be married some day. Even those with a clear-cut vocation, like doctors or nurses, cannot always remember the moment at which they knew themselves called, but simply found their minds made up, as I did.

Our early pictures of God are usually of someone friendly. This is true not only in happy families but even in families where there is some cruelty shown towards the children. Children in unhappy families seem to argue from the capriciousness of their own parents to the steady kindliness of God. Even in families where the name of God is deliberately excluded by the parents, I am fairly sure the children start out with a conviction that reality is friendly and dreams come true: only by degrees do they encounter hostility and unfairness and prejudice against themselves or against their friends. It is helpful to ask ourselves what was our mental picture of God when we were very young, and also what were our dreams for ourselves when we were children, because there is always a link between our early vision of ourselves and our eventual understanding of God. As life goes by we discover that God is in fact much more like our dream of ourselves than we could have dared to believe, not a stranger at all. I sometimes wonder whether those who as adults reject the notion of God are really rejecting the kind of person they themselves least wish to become, so that their working caricature of God is the exact opposite of the God they really believe in — they deny the negative, while cherishing the photograph.

We are born very vulnerable and dependent. As babies we can never be sure where the next meal is coming from, or when it will appear. We are carried in adults' hands, and we can never be sure we shall not be dropped. When we are in pain or discomfort, we can only cry, and hope that the adults will come and set us to rights again. When we are a little older we discover the word 'naughty' by painful experience, and we begin to fear lest perhaps if we are naughty enough we may be shut out of the house for ever or given away. In a well-organized family these fears of the baby are all contained, and they do not grow;

they go underground instead, reappearing at a later date, and in a different form. Just as I was taught about the golden bricks, and the false goal of competition for the love of God being given to us as six-year-olds, the same poisonous teaching may be instilled into other young minds and hearts even without any mention of God or religion. If children are taught that success *matters* to the core of their beings, that there are only a few places at the top, and getting one of them *matters* for personal growth, then long-buried fears will come to life again, and those near the top of the ladder of success will be under strain to stay there, and those near the bottom will begin quietly to despair.

But human beings are resilient, and the grace of God is at work in all of us, stronger than our fears. Children come through into adolescence with their most precious ideals intact, because those ideals, being from God, cannot be touched. There is more than one kind of prophet, and young people, today as always, champion many causes. They may often seem to be saying to human authority 'I will not serve', while in their own hearts they are trying to serve the truth. They feel themselves deeply called to serve their fellow human beings, especially those in trouble, though often they do not see that the call in their hearts is none other than God sending them out as prophets.

The labourers are few, as Jesus said. Young people look out on the world and marvel that so few the world over seem to care what happens to life's unfortunates. The young may not find Jesus to follow, but there are many causes and ideals and vocations in the world which are complementary to the work of Jesus, and one of those vocations they may find. They see the size of the problem and the dearth of volunteers, and they are determined to be part of the solution rather than part of the problem. They notice, even as adolescents, how some of the leaders in any calling lead simple lives and put service of the needy before their own personal profit. Justice is a virtue that matters a lot to young people: they want to see justice done in the world, and they want their own lives to be just. They hope to see the whole world put to rights in their own lifetime. All this of course was equally true of young people ten, twenty, thirty or however many years ago.

People who pray and people who do not consciously pray will normally go through much the same experiences as each other, but those who pray will find more serenity within their experiences. People who read the Scriptures and reflect on them

13

will find more meaning in their lives. To know oneself called by God is more inspiring than merely to want to do a thing, but the underlying experience may be the same in both cases. A bereavement is no less a bereavement, whether it happens to one who prays or one who does not pray, but the one who prays, and perhaps sees the sorrow as a cross to be carried with Jesus, has support from the sympathetic understanding of countless prayerful people who have been through the same ordeal. Even those who in their lives appear to be running away from God have religious experiences. Good-living Christians might be tempted to call one and the same experience a 'trial' when it happens to themselves, but a 'judgement' when it happens to others who appear to be less virtuous. What is called 'faithfulness' in their own case, being true to their convictions and so forth, may be called 'stubbornness' in another, and yet the reality in each case may be exactly the same.

When the time comes for young people to leave home and set about living a new life of their own choosing (or a life chosen for them by circumstances), they may well feel a certain nervousness, as I did, now that brave promises will have to be kept. In Christian terms, it is as if Jesus were striding out ahead on the journey to Jerusalem, and the disciples were hanging back. They have not yet received that inner fire of conviction which Jesus has, but he does not despise them on that account: he knows they will be given the fire in time.

'To those who prove victorious I will give . . . a white stone — a stone with *a new name* written on it, known only to the person who receives it' (Revelation 2:17). All our hidden lives have a great deal in common, but to each of us is given something unique. That quotation from the Book of Revelation calls up a picture of all people of all time standing in the presence of God, as many as the stars in the universe or the grains of sand on the seashores. God calls one name, and only one star, one grain of sand, one person knows who is being called. However similar we may all be, at our most precious centre each of us is unique. Instinctively we know this is true; what is more, this uniqueness is not something small within our ordinariness, but all-pervading, so that we are unique to our very fingertips. In the last resort, I cannot say how God appears to anybody else but myself. This treasure I may share to the best of my ability, mainly to help others find their own treasure.

14

II

Setting Out

1·THE START OF THE STEPS

I n the early summer of 1985 I once again found myself in Gibraltar, and the chance offered itself of climbing the Mediterranean Steps to the top of the Rock. The sky was hazy and the heat rather oppressive, because the wind known locally as the Levanter was blowing that day, an east wind which often brings cloud and gloom to the western side of the Rock where the city lies. I calculated that the steps on the eastern side would probably be enjoying some breeze, and the mist would take the fiercest of the sun from my back as I climbed, so that today was as good a day as any for my walk.

I set out on foot from the house where I was staying in the city, and passed the buildings where tourists may board the cable-car which takes them, by way of the hillside where the Barbary Apes live, to the summit. I was tempted to take a ride to the top and call off my walk, but the queue of holidaymakers was too long and the heat inside the station buildings unbearable, so I carried on walking, up through the ornamental gardens, up past the Casino, past the bishop's house, past the old people's home and so to the military guardpost near the southern end of the Rock. There the same signpost as before pointed along the dusty path towards the Mediterranean Steps.

I had my camera with me, and found it a good excuse for stopping every now and then to take a picture and to cool off. I remember telling myself that if the heat became impossible or the path looked really unsafe I would turn round and go home. But there was more excitement and interest about being on a real expedition, compared with the time before when I was simply spying out the land. I set out, with a fair amount of confidence that I would reach the top. As before, the going was level to start with, and as I came round following the path to the steep eastern side of the Rock, sure enough there was the breeze blowing pleasantly. Someone, I could not remember exactly who, had told me in the previous few days, that the steps would be in good repair, as it was not long since the engineers had checked them over. From the start of the path to the summit of the Steps I did not meet another soul,

15

and nobody knew where I had headed for this afternoon, so it was fairly important not to fall and have an accident.

All the way along the path, I could not see the ridge at the summit, as the cable-car passengers can see it from start to finish of their ride. Yet I was conscious of the summit and imagined the zig-zag sweep of the Steps ahead, even from the very beginning. Indeed it was the ambition to complete the walk and be at the summit which was stirring me to take each footstep as it came. On my right, down by the barracks, some troops were having rifle practice on a shooting range. The seagulls did not seem to mind the rattling guns — they were almost the only birds I saw on my climb. The flowers were more profuse now in early June than on my September visit previously. I wished I knew their names, but was able to capture a few of them with the camera. After about ten minutes' walking, I came again to the first of the steps. Not surprisingly, they led downhill as before; but this time, I followed them down, knowing I was on the only way to the top.

2·TWO YEARS' NOVICESHIP

In the late summer of 1952, at the age of eighteen, I arrived at the Jesuit novitiate at Harlaxton in Lincolnshire, along with some twenty other candidates. There were over twenty young men already there, about to start their second year, so we made a good number. We were to discover that although we were on trial for the two years of the novitiate, if we persevered we would be counted as Jesuits (members of the Society of Jesus, 'companions of Jesus') from the day we first arrived on the doorstep to become novices, not from the later date of our first vows. This knowledge gave us the comforting feeling that we were not simply candidates wanting to become companions of Jesus, but were already his companions. To be honest, I must admit that I had applied to join the novitiate half in hopes that God would indicate I was unsuitable for the life and would block my way. I would not have been heartbroken if the Master of Novices had told me I was in the wrong place: I think I would quite happily have taken his words as a sign of God's will and gone off to investigate what alternative God might have in mind. I know marriage would have been part of the alternative. However, the Master of Novices never said anything to me about going, and I found I was able to cope with the daily routine, so there I stayed. Hints given from time to time by fellow Jesuits make me think I was not alone in half hoping to be thrown out in the early years of my religious life.

Harlaxton Manor was at that time the place of the noviceship of the English Province (now known as the British Province) of the Society of Jesus. We newcomers got a shock when we saw the building: we knew that God's prophets do not live in palaces, yet here was a palace of a place — Grantham Palace was one of its titles. We soon discovered, though, that the students' living quarters were very simple: we had cubicles not rooms, desks in a common (and silent) dormitory, wash-bowls and jugs rather than running hot and cold water. Where we lived had formerly been either the servants' quarters, or in some cases the stables, of the manor house.

The company was delightful. One small example stays in my mind, of how kind everybody was: at table, or whenever any good things were being passed around, the best place to be was at the end of the line, because the people who came first always left the best things for those who were to follow. They really did: the sheer surprise of it gives me pleasure still. Also I found myself on the receiving end of what was still an ideal with me, in that we were all encouraged to be content with whatever companion we found ourselves beside, rather than seek out others we might find more congenial. I who had since schooldays wanted to be 'friend of all the world', found an official blessing on that old ideal being given within my chosen new life. On a walk, or at recreation or anywhere, companions were chosen at random, and I found it heartwarming to be greeted and welcomed as a friend by the companions chosen for me, and to know I could rely on that friendship.

The order of the day usually followed these lines: early rise; private prayer; Mass; breakfast; housework; a talk from the Novice Master, Father George Walkerley; study; dinner; in the afternoon, games or gardening or a walk; tea; spiritual reading; private prayer; supper; recreation; night prayer. Every now and then we had a whole day off for a long walk, and these days I loved. I had never lived in the country before, and some of the other novices were countrymen who could point out a thousand things I would never have noticed for myself. I was particularly happy to learn to identify many birds, and some birdcalls. Also, living in the country for the first time I became very much aware of the seasons changing, and how long the winter is. Every little sign of spring became precious. In the early autumn we did a fair amount of fruit-picking. We saw, too, how the birds and small animals fitted their lives in with the seasons.

In the house, with its community of fifty or so, there was no domestic help from outside, everything was done by the Jesuits. Some of the chores — like washing-up, laying tables, sweeping, dusting, preparing vegetables — most of us had been accustomed to helping with at home. For my part, I found polishing floors and keeping the lavatories gleaming clean were two new experiences. Serving at table was fairly novel as well: a few of us would be chosen by turns to wait on everyone else and then have our own meal afterwards. I had come in order to be of service to God, and these tasks which had once been done by servants in that big house seemed an appropriate way to start.

We had our first practice in giving sermons, and in having our sermons criticized! Another activity which I enjoyed was bookbinding — sometimes of an afternoon instead of manual work outdoors we had manual work indoors, and my first and favourite workshop was the bookbindery, where we learned how to repair damaged but still useful books from the library: to take them to pieces, restitch, recut and rebind them. I also very much enjoyed the Sunday afternoon 'catechism classes' we ran for the parish priest in Grantham, three miles away. I was given what you might call the remedial class or what I secretly called the waifs and strays: children who could not be fitted in conveniently with the other classes, because they were too young, too shy or too far behind in knowledge. I learnt a lot of good things from them, so I hope they learnt something good from me.

All in all the novitiate had closely packed days, with every minute organized, and a lot of changing from one activity to another. I liked it; I liked the way I could be sure at any given moment that I was where God wanted me to be, doing what he wanted me to do. In later stages of my training when I would have more decisions of my own to make, I might wonder if this minute-by-minute regime of the novitiate was the best preparation for a busy life with more responsibility; but at the time it was peace and balm to my soul, since all other roads were closed and I had just the one well-marked path to walk, knowing that it led to God. I had come to the Jesuits desiring to 'help God' in whatever service he might indicate, and here he was indicating more or less minute

by minute what he wanted. We were beginners, so it was not for
us to question openly the time-honoured system, particularly as
Father Walkerley was in advance of his time as a director. I could
see better men than I getting on with the daily routine, so I just
relaxed and enjoyed being so close to God.

Only a few weeks after our arrival at Harlaxton we were
plunged into the full *Spiritual Exercises* of St Ignatius Loyola,
founder of the 'companions of Jesus'. From the time of our arrival
we had been coached so as to be able to pray for ten minutes,
half an hour, an hour at a time without giving up. Thus armed
we were guided through thirty days' retreat, a time of silence
and prayer, following the *Spiritual Exercises* The second, third
and fourth weeks of St Ignatius's plan involve praying one's
way through the gospels, contemplating first the childhood and
public life of Jesus, then his passion, then his resurrection. The
ideal of 'service' is one of the foundation stones of the *Exercises*,
so again I felt at home: Ignatius himself had formerly been
in the service of a duke as one of his retainers, wearing the
duke's livery, fighting his battles and being maintained and if
necessary, protected by him. In the *Exercises* we see, and are
invited to follow, the way Ignatius transferred his allegiance
to Jesus his new king, how he desired to give loyal and out-
standing service to him, wearing his livery, fighting his battles
alongside him, accepting his mercy and protection, and then
offering this service with Christ to the Father who serves us
all.

One of the prayers Father Walkerley introduced us to in the
course of the thirty days, and which has remained a firm favourite with me ever since, is the prayer of St Richard of Chichester:
'. . . My Lord Jesus Christ, . . . most merciful Redeemer, Friend
and Brother, may I know thee more clearly, love thee more dearly,
and follow thee more nearly'. The most precious long-term effect
of these thirty days is that ever afterwards on reading about, hearing about or praying about any of these mysteries of the life of
Christ I have the same feeling as about an event I had actually
witnessed – I feel as if I had been there. The reason must be, that
Jesus is real, still saying the same words and doing the same actions. The disappointing side-effect is that ever afterwards these
mysteries *are* in a sense memories, and I cannot recapture the
novelty of the first hour or hours spent imagining them taking
place all around me.

A few months after the Long Retreat I experienced something which will take longer to describe than it took to happen. One evening we were all at our desks for spiritual reading. I was reading St Luke's gospel, at the point where Jesus entered a certain village, I think the one where he went to stay with Martha and Mary. I was reading the gospel in Latin, as one of the suggestions made to us had been that we read the familiar gospels in an unfamiliar version so as to keep our minds awake to what was written there. The Latin Vulgate version of 'he entered a certain village' was *intravit quoddam castellum*, and suddenly I knew that Jesus had that instant entered a certain 'castle', my castle, my interior castle. (I had not read the book *The Interior Castle*, by the sixteenth-century Carmelite nun and mystic St Teresa of Avila, but I knew the title.) This entering of my interior castle by Jesus was utterly real, infinitely more real than anything I had called real in my life before. In that moment I knew that my gamble in joining the Society of Jesus and signing my life away had paid off. Jesus was real, Jesus was alive, Jesus was risen, Jesus was there in the room with me, Jesus was within me.

Soon afterwards, still in my first year at Harlaxton, I chose a motto for myself. Father Walkerley had suggested to us that if we found the idea helpful we could each choose a motto and try to live up to it, the sort of word or phrase that would go well inscribed under the shield on a coat-of-arms. I do not think I hesitated at all: as soon as I put my mind to the question I chose the words *En servus tuus*, 'Behold, your servant', from that other great manual of spiritual devotion, the *Imitation of Christ* (Book III, Chapter 15). In its setting the quotation reads: 'Lord, you know what is best. . . . Give what you wish, and as much as you wish, and when you wish. Do with me as you know best, and as best pleases you, and is most for your honour. Put me where you wish, and deal with me freely in all matters. I am in your hand; turn me backwards, turn me forwards, turn me upside down. Behold, your servant am I, ready for anything.'

There was one more sudden experience of the reality and presence of Jesus before I left the novitiate. This time I was reading St Luke in English, the passage about the rich man who had the poor man Lazarus lying at his gate. When I read those words 'at his gate', suddenly I was the rich man, the gate was the gate of my senses, the poor man was at one and the same time Jesus and my brethren who were at the gate of my senses all day long. Later on I interpreted and extended the initial truth to include not just those I saw with my own eyes and heard with my own ears but also those I read about and heard about; but I think the original impact was the truer one. Again, I *knew* Jesus was there: the knowledge was over in an instant, but I was unbelievably happy for two days afterwards, and the memory has been a source of strength and consolation ever since.

The sudden moments of illumination still did not alter the fact that during those two years as a novice, I continued living by the Old Testament rather than the New, in spite of daily Mass, daily reading from the gospels and other New Testament books, long daily periods of prayer, and careful initiation into the ways of Christian religious life. I was still scrupulous, and I suspect I was not the only one — the house's new kitten was christened Scruples and the name stuck! I still feared, deep down, that if I did not measure up, God would stop loving me, that his love was conditional.

Just three small dints were made in my thick armour of fear. The first was when the Novice Master in one of his morning talks spent a while on the prayer that began in Latin *Nobis quoque peccatoribus* in the Ordinary part of the Mass: 'For ourselves too, your servants, we ask some share in the fellowship of your apostles and martyrs . . . and with all the saints, *though we are sinners*. We trust (not in our merits, but) only in your mercy and love. Let us into their company, not as a measurer of merit, but as a generous giver-out of pardon.' I forget the exact translation he used, but he brought out the daringness, the cheekiness even, of this prayer the western Church had used daily for some seventeen centuries. He told us to think about it as we prayed it each day; I have loved that prayer from that day to this.

The second dint in my armour came from a story in a translation from one of the Desert Fathers, those early Christians, many of them followers of St Anthony, who went to live in great austerity as solitary monks and hermits in the Egyptian desert. This was the story of an old monk who had been all his life most lax about keeping the rule of the monastery. On his deathbed he was asked by the Abbot how come he looked so serene, seeing he was shortly to meet his judge. The old man replied that Jesus had appeared to him and reassured him. All his life he had never judged anyone, so Jesus was not going to judge him either. From the day of my first hearing that story I began to take special care not to judge anyone. The third dint in my armour was delivered by a reading from one of the Fathers of the Church, writing in the early centuries of Christianity, who said that there are not two ways before us, the way of good and the way of evil, but one road only, and we either face up it towards God or down it away from him. And — here was the big shock for me — he said that no matter how far sinners have gone down the road away from God, all they have to do to be saved is to turn round and face him again. I thought they would at least have to struggle back up the road to where they started, but no – all they had to do was turn around where they stood. I have since tried without success to trace that passage and identify the writer, but the beauty of what he said does not depend on his name, I suppose.

The spirit of competition was there among us students, the spirit of vying for God's favour and attention, but it was sub-merged. We all got up at the same time, prayed for the same length of time, worked for the same time, attended the same talks and had no examinations to distinguish between us. We were encouraged not to discuss with one another our inner feelings or how we were coping with the hours of prayer. I say the spirit of competition was there because in the years that immediately followed I, for one, grew unduly depressed at what I considered my failure in prayer and study and the religious life in general. If we could have been taught to cope with the difference in talents between us openly, in the sight of a God who loves failures as much as successes, perhaps the years ahead might not have been so painful. But then, can anyone hear the Good News before his ears are opened? Perhaps I was simply deaf to what was being said all along. As the time drew near for leaving Harlaxton and moving on to the next stage of training, Father Walkerley — for whom I had great affection as well as admiration — did try to warn us about the dangers we would encounter, but it was always danger from others of the community, the danger of being swayed by the bad example of the over-confident, by those who felt they had no longer any need of prayer — that sort of thing. He did not seem to warn us about the enemy within, the fear of failing as God's servant which is a thousand times more deadly than failure itself. Only Jesus himself could crush that enemy.

We made our vows, our promises to remain in this Company of Jesus to the end of our days as far as in us lay, at a simple ceremony in 1954, two years and a day after our arrival, and in the same house, Harlaxton Manor. I found it deeply disappointing that neither our families nor any Jesuits from other houses were invited. I have the impression sometimes that my family thought the most unnatural thing about those two years was that I who used to play the piano for hours at a time at home was asked not to play it at all for the whole two years; but to me the most unnatural thing was that they were not invited to the vow ceremony. Happy to relate, in the present-day noviceship parents, brothers and sisters are invited to the vows as well as at other times, novices may go home occasionally, and musicians are encouraged to keep up their skills. As it happens, I found I could play rather better after the enforced two years' rest than I could before.

3·'THIS IS THE GATE OF HEAVEN'

Among the Scripture passages that were important to me in the two years I spent as a novice, I could mention first of all the psalms and canticles of praise, especially the 'Song of the three young men' from Daniel 3.52–90 (or, in some Bibles, included in the Apocrypha) which I tried to learn by heart. In spite of a fair amount of surface tension in my days — in the days of all of us there, where novices were defined as people who laughed and broke things — there was a deep happiness which came of being in the right place, so I felt like praising God. That canticle had a verse for every beautiful creature in the world of nature, from the sun and moon down to the frosts and the dew, to all of which I was closer than I had ever been before.

We were aware of the foundation in Scripture for our learning to accept warmly whoever might turn up as a companion for a walk or for recreation: 'In so far as you did this to one of the least of these brothers of mine, you did it to me' (Matthew 25:40). And when we waited at meals and had our own meal afterwards we remembered how Jesus had said, through the master in his parable, 'Get my supper laid; make yourself tidy and wait on me while I eat and drink. You can eat and drink yourself afterwards' (Luke 17:8). And when we had done all we had been told to do of the serving or any other form of work, we learned not to look for thanks or praise. 'Say, "We are merely servants: we have done no more than our duty"' (Luke 17:10).

23

Mary the mother of Jesus said to the servants at Cana, 'Do whatever he tells you' (John 2:5). I think we all of us at Harlaxton found it easy to take our prayers and requests to Mary and then go with her to Jesus (cf. John 2:1–4) as St Ignatius taught us to do with important requests during the *Spiritual Exercises*. Those few words of Mary's, 'Do whatever he tells you', were interpreted by me at least as meaning 'Do whatever is next on the agenda, as if Jesus himself had told you to do it'.

Jesus was for his disciples at once Lord, Teacher and, at least by implication, Master, since 'a disciple is not above his teacher, nor a servant above his master' (Matthew 10:24) as he told them, and it was only at the Last Supper he said to them 'I shall not call you servants any more . . . I call you friends' (John 15:15). During our two years of instruction I had a distinct and warm feeling of what it must have been like for Jesus' disciples, especially on the occasions when he took them to one side or went apart from the crowd with them into the house, and they asked him questions about his recent words or actions (e.g. Mark 9:28). We were not taught academic subjects during this time, only the art of living as a servant and companion of Jesus. As we 'have only one Teacher, the Christ' (Matthew 23:10) anything of lasting value we learnt in that time must have been taught by him. And though, as I have said, I still secretly wondered which among us was the greatest (cf. Mark 9:34), I did know well that we had come 'not . . . to be served but to serve' (Mark 10:45), following Jesus' own example as summed up by his action at the Last Supper in washing his disciples' feet (cf. John 13:15).

The gospel passages and other Scripture passages dwelt on in the course of the *Spiritual Exercises* are too many to list. I would only recall that in most of them St Ignatius directs exercitants to imagine themselves into the gospel scene, finding some excuse for being there, as it were. Very often I found myself, as countless others including Ignatius himself have done, in imagination taking the part of a servant in the scene, trying to make myself useful at the stable in Bethlehem, helping to give out loaves and fishes on the hillside in Galilee, helping to fetch the donkey for Jesus' entry into Jerusalem, or again helping Peter and John prepare the room for the Passover.

At times the power and majesty of God seemed so great that I thought of myself rather as his slave than as his servant. How wonderful to be like a sword in his hand or an arrow in his quiver (cf. Isaiah 49:2)! How good to be able to recognize the least indication of his finger, like the slaves and slave-girl in the psalm, their eyes fixed on the hand of their master or mistress (cf. Psalm 123:1f.)! My favourite psalm for a time was Psalm 119, the longest one in the book, because in every one of its 176 verses it delights in the will of God, using many synonyms for 'will' such as 'your decrees, your Law, your ways, your precepts, your statutes, your every commandment, your rules of righteousness, your promises, your word'. I liked it because it seemed to fit in with our busy switching from one activity to another while following always only God's will: 'I am your servant; if you will explain, I shall embrace your decrees' (verse 125). Later I was to feel lost because every activity was no longer mapped out for us, but at this time I found the long psalm very helpful. I was probably praying it like a good Pharisee, an upholder of the Law of Moses rooted in the Old Testament, because I felt secure within these decrees (laws, ways, precepts etc., etc.) as if God would love me for keeping them. Carried along by the general enthusiasm, I never really thought how it would be if I were to stray from the narrow guidelines. Perhaps I didn't get as far as the very last verse, which begins: 'I am wandering like a lost sheep: come and look for your servant . . .' (verse 176).

St Ignatius in the *Exercises* writes about consolation from God that comes through ordinary channels, and consolation from God that comes direct, 'without previous cause', out of the blue. The two sudden moments I have mentioned, about Jesus entering the 'castle' and the poor man Lazarus at my gate, were of this second kind of consolation, sudden as lightning and yet as gentle as must have been Jesus' entry into the upper room when the doors were closed (cf. John 20:19). Those two consolations did not teach me any new truth: after all, we each received into ourselves Christ present in the Eucharist every day, and we already knew that he was present in each one of us for the others to love; but they did greatly strengthen my conviction about the reality of Jesus, both in myself and in my neighbour. I cannot help thinking that consolations of this kind are rather like a gift from God of a bullet-proof vest, indicating that bullets will be flying before long and the wearer will need all the protection he can wear. Comparable perhaps is the way the angel of Yahweh came to the farmer Gideon as he was threshing his wheat in secret for fear of the enemy, and said, 'Yahweh is with you, valiant warrior'. The great military hero who delivered Israel from the Midianites was no warrior at all until the angel spoke to him (cf. Judges 6:12). Another effect of these two consolations was to give me renewed confidence in the dreams, visions and angels mentioned in the Scriptures: if God could in less time than it takes to tell give me complete conviction that Jesus is alive, then he could certainly give messages to all those great servants of his as described in the Old and New Testament writings. I, too, in my own way, felt like saying about our house in Harlaxton 'For me "this is . . . a house of God; this is the gate of heaven"', along with Jacob after his dream (cf. Genesis 28:27).

In my prayers I still thought of Jesus as 'over there' and of myself as 'here', he beside me, I beside him, rather than he within me. I loved the beautiful verse, 'Look, I am standing at the door, knocking. If one of you hears me calling and opens the door, I will come in to share his meal, side by side with him' (Revelation 3:20), telling him often that my door was open. I knew now that Jesus is alive, but I think he must have been saying to me, as he once said to the city of Jerusalem, 'If you . . . had only understood on this day the message of peace! But, alas, it is hidden from your eyes!' (Luke 19:42), since I had really not yet understood the Good News. I did treasure, on account of the story of the old monk, the message that would in the end bring me peace: 'Do not judge, and you will not be judged yourselves' (Luke 6:37). My favourite psalm of all was Psalm 34, and my favourite verses within the psalm were:

'I will bless Yahweh at all times . . .' (verse 1)
and
'Come, my children, listen to me . . .' (verse 11)
and
'Yahweh is near to the broken hearted,
he helps those whose spirit is crushed' (verse 18).

4·FINDING WHAT OUR HEART DESIRES

First of all, I would not want anyone to think I look on the life of a layperson as being comparable to a cable-car to heaven whereas I had to climb on foot! All I was implying was that any of us on the threshold of a chosen way of life may suddenly see the alternatives as being more attractive, but this does not mean we have chosen wrongly. Similarly, when I said that I realized my gamble had come off, and I had not signed away my life for nothing, I was not wishing to hint that the religious life is the only way to God, but merely that the religious life is a more unfortunate choice than most, if Christ has not been raised. Since Christ has been raised, there is joy for all Christians, and their sacrifices for the sake of goodness and truth are not made in vain.

This time in my life, then, is parallel to the time in anyone's life when they are blessed in finding what their heart desires — students following the subject they love, young married couples setting up house, people finding their first job and liking it, any person young or old whom disillusionment has not yet touched. A wise director once said to me that the surest vocation from God is one which comes to us without our realizing it at first, rather than the vocation that depends on some sudden 'call'. Those who are sure and happy in what they are doing have therefore nearly every minute of every day mapped out for them, just as any novice has in religious life. Their vocation, their job, their duties at home are all pretty obvious. They too may have hidden in their hearts a competitiveness which will not surface until they either forge ahead in their career (in which case others notice it before they notice it themselves), or else they begin to fall behind their hopes and expectations for themselves. Somewhere, before our days are over, we all have to learn that we each like a star have our own shining, our own brilliance which no one can take away from us, ever.

Those who find themselves attracted by prayer, and who try to pray for a certain amount of time every day or every week will almost certainly find, as I found and as, I think, all of us novices found, that the first excitement of praying wears off. We made the effort, doing our best, of praying several hours a day through

27

those thirty days, and then for two or three hours a day for the rest of the novitiate, but that effort just brought us sooner to the stage where imagination was not so much of a help. Luckily, we were reassured on all sides that trying to pray is equal in every respect to praying, even if (as a little book by Father Leonard Boase puts it) the effort of concentration may seem like trying to balance a ping-pong ball on the top of a fountain-jet of water. Father Boase reckoned — we liked his book as novices — that if two or three times in a half-hour you 'woke up' and tried to get back to what you had planned to pray about, then you were doing well. Moreover, it was quite normal for prayer to be like that for the rest of one's life.

III
Breakdown

1·THE STEPS DOWNWARD – AND DANGEROUS CORNERS

The steps down were large and clumsy, a foot deep at times. The old murmuring began to come back to my mind: if this was the size of them going down, they would be even more trouble to me coming back up again, should I have to turn round. There was another sensation besides, which I had not expected. The engineers had only put safety barriers at the more obviously dangerous corners and cliff-edges, but there were several other stretches of the path where I had the sensation of stepping off into nothing. Balance has never been one of my greatest skills, and to look down on my right side and see the land slope steeply to the edge of a cliff was a little unnerving.

On my left the bulk of the Rock came closer and closer, until the path was descending right under a cliff one or two hundred feet high. The cliff face looked clean, as if there was no danger of any rocks falling unexpectedly, but even so I do not like walking under cliffs: they seem to contain a menace to anyone who walks there. What with the steep slopes down to my right and the cliff up to my left and above me, there was nothing for it but to keep my eyes fixed on the path and its steps ahead of me. Of the two sides, I found the overhanging cliff on the left much the more threatening.

The path ahead was none too encouraging, either. I had gone down so many steps by this time that I was beginning seriously to wonder if the path was not going to land me back at sea-level, on the road which runs along the foot of the Rock by the sea on the eastern side. Did it go down to the road, and then lead on to quite another path climbing to the top? Had I heard aright, about this path I was on being the one that led to the summit? Was this the one the troops had recently repaired? Here I was, hot, sticky, eyes glued down, disappointed at not climbing upwards as I had hoped to be by this time. I could not even look up, for fear of this blessed cliff on my left. But I did carry on walking, because this was what I had decided to do, and there would be no point in turning round and going home, leaving my questions still unanswered.

2·THE 'SCHOLASTIC' YEARS – AND INABILITY TO OBEY

After the day of our vows at Harlaxton, most of us younger students moved to a college in Roehampton, near London, for a year of general studies before going on to philosophy. We were to revise the subjects we had chiefly studied at school, and keep them if possible at a level suitable for university entrance later; we also studied, in a leisurely fashion, the kind of subjects we had passed over at school – so that I having studied chiefly classics was given a very welcome introduction to physics, chemistry and biology; thirdly, we embarked on this year as the first year of a teacher-training course. A fourth purpose was that of helping us to switch from the rather hot-house atmosphere of the novitiate to the ordinary life of a student . . . but a student in a religious community.

The 'gentleman's course' in the sciences I found fascinating. The lecturers were experts at popularizing their subjects, with the result that we had many of the joys of science with hardly any toil. From the physics I chiefly recall the sheer simplicity of the great theories like the law of gravity and the theory of relativity: reality seems immensely complicated, until some genius sees one law governing all. What most impressed me in chemistry was the way the table of elements is built up — again a seemingly confused reality but with a simple pattern behind the whole, and every element the sum of its own number of protons and neutrons. In biology what has stayed in my imagination is the spiral structure of genes and chromosomes whereby every cell of each human body contains the master plan of that person's characteristics, so that if my finger is cut, both nearby and distant cells follow the master plan for healing my finger to its original shape. I found most amazing the way cells of the male and of the female divide within themselves, and realign with one another to form a new creature; yet each new child has a different genetic make-up from its siblings. Some understanding also stayed in my mind of how it comes about that a weakness can at times be carried through one or more generations of a family before reappearing in a child of a later generation.

Living at Roehampton, with a view over Richmond Park, we must have had one of the most pleasant situations in the whole of London, but I always felt a certain claustrophobia, being conscious that London just went on and on, district after district, town after town, for many miles more. I used to yearn for a good, breezy Lancashire hillside with hardly anyone in sight. For me the best thing about London was the art galleries, especially the National Gallery and the Tate. They were free, which was just as well, as our spending money for a day out only covered the bus and train fare to and from town. My favourite picture was *The Madonna of the Meadow* by Giovanni Bellini: I sat in front of it by the hour. There is something utterly serene about the composition of figures and landscape, and I found sitting there as refreshing as a picnic with dear friends and no flies. I also discovered the fascination of Rembrandt, whose paintings I had always found rather sombre in reproductions: now it was possible to look into the eyes and face of one of his self-portraits and find one's own eyes and face looking back, as from a mirror, but unfathomably enriched by the artist. I think his paintings do that for anyone fortunate enough to stand in front of them. Vincent van Gogh was another of my favourites, for the blaze of colour and the swirling vision.

One moment in the Tate Gallery I am particularly proud of. My companion that day was less at home amidst the modern art than he was among the classical paintings. As we entered one gallery he looked across at a fairly small painting on the far wall and said something like: 'Really! some of these paintings are rubbish, meaningless. Now what on earth is that one over there supposed to represent? Nothing!' I told him, from where I stood it looked like a man tying his shoelace. Sure enough, we went over to it and it is entitled *Man tying his shoelace*. My companion was unsure whether to believe me when I said quite truthfully I had never seen the painting before. Of the abstract art I found the constructions of Naum Gabo the most thrilling, nylon string and Perspex mostly, the string wound round the Perspex in the manner of railings seen through railings.

One of the less pleasant experiences of this year for me was being choirmaster for our small group of first-year students. I had loved being in the choir both at school and as a novice, but was almost totally at sea having to organize and prepare the singing of other people. In the matter of writing and English composition, however, I came on quite well. I even wrote a one-act play, for the first and only time in my life, and my companions were kind enough to learn the parts and put it on at a party one day. I can hardly remember anything about it now, except that it taught me how a playwright may be resolving his own frustrations while seeming to resolve those of the characters in the play.

The year in London drew to a close. I think we all felt a certain dissatisfaction with it: for my part, I was to find it had cocooned us too much, kept us too sheltered, so that we still had before us the change of gear into being self-reliant students in a religious community, just as if we had never had the year in London. Soon after our time this kind of buffer year was abandoned, and students went straight from noviceship to philosophy.

In September of 1955, then, my contemporaries and I moved to Heythrop College in Oxfordshire to start the three-year course in Scholastic Philosophy.

All around Heythrop was countryside enough for anyone, but still not much in the way of hills. However, as it turned out, the philosophy itself was more than enough of a climb for me. Several years later, during my studies in theology, one of the lecturers re-assured me about philosophy: about one in ten of human beings, he said, is a born philosopher and able to cope with philosophical thinking; the rest may go through the motions, but no amount of study will turn them into real philosophers. From the whole of the three years' course I seem to have retained only three crumbs of comfort, though as crumbs they went a long way. The first had the unpromising title of 'futurables', the second was the story of the stars, and the third was one of St Thomas Aquinas's 'five ways' of 'proving' the existence of God.

As regards the 'futurables', this was a portmanteau title for all the things that might have been in our lives, had we only acted differently. In our course in 'natural theology' (that is, what philosophy can say about God) I was totally convinced by the lectures, once and for all in my mind if not yet in my heart, that those 'might have beens' have no existence in the mind of God. He is entirely content with what is, content to let bygones be bygones and take *what is* as his starting point. As I now like to put it to myself, when I go astray God as a good shepherd does not sit sulking in the place where I ought to be; he is there in the place where I am, ready to gather me up in his arms. As regards the stars, the course in cosmology tied in with some private reading I was doing, about the size of the universe — how far away the moon, the sun, the stars and star clusters, the next nearest galaxy, out to the galaxies human beings will never see. The one of St Thomas's 'five ways' which appealed deeply to me was the argument from the presence of design in nature to the presence of God as designer.

I did not mind being unable to cope with the mysteries of time and space, but I did find it very frustrating not being able to cope with the concepts of scholastic or (a little) modern philosophy, which were supposed to be our bread and butter for these three years. It fell to my lot to produce the students' New Year play in my third year. A small committee of us had ambitions to put on one of Ben Jonson's comedies, and for personal reasons I chose to do *The Alchemist*, in which the playwright pours scorn on the private Latin language used by the alchemist and his colleagues and assistants while all the time the whole business of alchemy was a hollow sham. Many of the Latin phrases in the play are taken straight from scholastic philosophy, and in choosing it I suppose I was trying to tell everyone how bitterly disappointed I was in the whole course of philosophy as it was presented to us. My sympathies go out to the principal actors, who did a marvellous job with page after page of blank verse!

Next came another of those lights straight from heaven. I was on my own one winter evening in the philosophy students' chapel, praying my way around the fourteen Stations of the Cross, those plaques on the wall of Catholic churches and chapels representing fourteen stages of the Way from Jesus' being condemned by Pilate to his burial. I can remember exactly where I was standing, when I suddenly understood far more than could be told in the same time. The Father was at the end of the way, Jesus was by my side and we were going to the Father. What was behind us was nothing to worry about. Between the Father and the Son was a homesickness, a Homesickness — the Spirit. The one homesickness was shared by the Father (wanting his Son back) and the Son (wanting to be back with the Father). One and the same homesickness reached from the crown of the Father's head (so to speak) to the furthest heel of the Son (so to speak) and back again, and everywhere between.

I was beside Jesus, but the same homesickness touched me as well. I felt as if I was taken up into this magnetism between Father and Son. Later on I used the illustration of two powerful magnets my brother and I once had at home: to our surprise they would not pick up certain metals. There in the philosophers' chapel it was as if Jesus in his saving work has so mixed his imperishable metal with our mortal selves, that his divine magnetism, his divine homesickness, runs through us as well. Like little coins that were previously impervious to that homesickness, we now share it, and cling as alloyed metals to the side of Jesus. In so far as there was any picture going with all this sudden clarity in my mind, it was of the father of the prodigal son, and the son starting off home.

I recalled, then, how Father Clifford Howell, who used our novitiate house as his home base and occasionally gave us an inspiring talk on the Church's liturgy, had startled me by hinting that we should not adore the Blessed Sacrament as the End of the Journey, but only as the Way. He had also made us look at the words we already heard or spoke in the Mass, which almost exclusively pray to the Father through the Son. Something clicked into place in my mind and heart, that evening as I was following the Way of the Cross; all the puzzling sayings of Jesus in St John's gospel about his Father and the Spirit and himself were suddenly not so puzzling, but more like invitations: 'Now you know where you stand. From your new standpoint, look again at what you have read before.'

One final thing I would say about that homesickness, before moving on with my story: it is a homesickness, or more properly a *homing instinct*, which becomes part of us, so that we can tell our way home even in the dark or if apparently separated from our leader.

*   *   *

Gradually as the three years of philosophy went by, I *did* feel in the dark and separated from my leader. It was a question of not being able to keep up, with the studies first of all. For the first time in my life, almost, I was not 'top of the class', nor anywhere near it. That would not have been so bad, if only I had been able to understand or love or enjoy the studies in the various branches of philosophy, but I only got the marks I did get in the examinations by learning off the required responses. There was no joy, and yet these three long years were supposed to be preparing me to be an apostle in the world of men and women. Moreover, I knew Jesus had called me here. So I felt deeply that he had gone on ahead, but I could not keep up with him.

If I found no joy in philosophy, I found a lot of joy in other reading, to which I turned more and more frequently. To keep the classical studies from going rusty, I read a lot of texts, of which my firm favourites were the *Odyssey* of Homer and the comedies of Aristophanes as well as the Greek tragic plays. We had oceans of time to ourselves, there in the Oxfordshire countryside with hardly any apostolic outlets, so I happily read through the whole of Shakespeare's plays, the whole of Chaucer's works and Milton's poems. Reading *Paradise Lost* at that time did not help the way I was feeling. A book which was first published about the time of my philosophy course was *The Lord of the Rings* by J. R. R. Tolkien. Nearly all of us students read it with fascination, and I can remember identifying with the hero as he struggles deeper and deeper into darkness because of a homing instinct within him. Come to that, the line which I can remember more vividly than any other in Shakespeare is about darkness:

> *If I must die,*
> *I will encounter darkness as a bride,*
> *And hug it in mine arms.*
>
> (*Measure for Measure* III, 1, 81)

Of course, the longer I spent on literature, the more guilty I felt about not making sense of philosophy. All unawares, I was under the strong spell of competitiveness: I had to be out in front of everybody, or else I went to pieces and said the game was stupid, and I wasn't playing any more. Yet secretly I still longed to be good at philosophy. This tension was the first cause of my breakdown. Deep inside, I was the Servant wanting to do the Master's will and do it well: a lengthy training I could cope with, so long as it was providing me with the tools of the trade for the future. But this philosophy made little or no sense to me, so was I in the right place, as deep down I knew I was? It was all very confusing. To make matters worse, we used to team up with one other student to go over the material of each lecture, and I was supposed to be the stronger partner; so I felt all the time that I was letting my partner down, not being able to simplify the subject enough for him.

Then there was the absence of people to preach to. In all the three years at Heythrop, my only outlet as an apostle was a weekly bicycle ride to a tiny village of two houses, there to give a Sunday school to two little boys and to have a chat with their parents. My turn at this lasted for a year, then another student took over. My life's journey to date seemed a long way to come for so little. Nowadays, thirty years later, the philosophy students have much wider opportunities for working with people in the city outside the newly-sited college, and this I feel sure can only be good for them. The feeling of isolation from 'the fields of the harvest' was a second cause of stress leading to breakdown.

Then there was the discovery that I could no longer keep up with the ways of praying, of spiritual reading, examination of conscience twice a day, reflection and so forth, now that faithfulness was more a matter left to ourselves and we were not doing everything at the same time as each other. Here again was the spirit of competition, which for me turned out to be a false god. Instead of being content with the quality and quantity of what I could cope with, I fell to imagining how far ahead the others must be leaping in the spiritual life, leaving me lagging behind. Father Walkerley had warned us about bad example from students who had ceased to care about their calling, but here at Heythrop were fine men who cut corners. Now I did not know how to cut corners without feeling unbearably guilty, and I did not know how to carry on without cutting corners. In the end, I think it was the daily hour of prayer that I clung to, and let the rest go. But the struggle over this was another cause of breakdown.

The next factor in the breakdown had to do with relationships with my colleagues, my fellow students. As I have mentioned more than once, I had a great ambition to be friend of everyone, all things to everybody, and not the exclusive friend of a few. Yet as soon as we reached Heythrop we found ourselves, as if by a chemical change, being drawn into this group or that group, which distressed me no end. Next I found myself looking to have one or two close friends myself, but that was not a good idea either, since I felt guilty all the time at betraying my vision. Looking back, I would say I am too susceptible or suggestible by nature to have very close friends. I have to follow my own star, and the too close presence of others dazzles my eyes and makes me lose my sense of direction.

*　*　*

I hope what I have written about my three years at Heythrop does not sound cynical. I was often called cynical in those days, but cynicism is a trait that goes with high ideals, too high ideals in fact. A cynic is one who has failed, so he thinks, to live up to his own high ideals. If he had abandoned his ideals, he would not be cynical any more. Like the two disciples on the road to Emmaus, who had high hopes of Jesus but thought they had been let down, most cynics are closer than they think to the coming of light and warmth.

The final trigger that set off the explosion of my breakdown was a philosophical essay. I forget now what it was about, but we had so many days to finish it off. I began well enough, but about half-way through I seemed to have a breakthrough, in fact I seemed to have discovered the secret of the universe, and it was Oh, so simple. I wrote, and I wrote, and I could not stop writing — until somebody discovered I was seriously ill. I was taken to the college infirmary, and there for a whole week I did not sleep at all. Because of my mental condition, it never occurred to me to tell anyone I had not slept for a week; when the truth did slip out, more or less by accident, I was taken into a hospital in Oxford. I can remember trying to work out, as we drove to Oxford in the minibus, what all these other students and priests were coming with me for, and being rather disappointed when they got out first and went about their free day activities. I alone was going to hospital.

I imagine there is no need to detail the ways in which patients suffering from nervous breakdowns are first coped with and then healed in hospital. I was there for about a month in all. There were visits from people in college and from my own family, but I can remember very little beyond the fact that they happened. After the month I was discharged from hospital and taken home by my parents to convalesce. I can remember the shock and the puzzlement along with the love and concern in their eyes and faces; the same, too, in the faces of my brother and sister, with both of whom I spent some time. The hospital people had apparently told my father the cure might not last, but the recurrence happened only about a month after my leaving Oxford. Once again I started flying high as a kite, as the saying goes, and my father, who was a doctor, a general practitioner, took me to another hospital, near Manchester, and I was admitted there.

Again the first task of the hospital was to calm me down, a task they performed with an alarming efficiency. If the dominant thought of my first breakdown was that I had discovered the secret of the universe, the key thought of this second breakdown was that I had escaped — escaped from the tyranny of trying to keep up. The pressure on me had been too great, and I had snapped — but now the pressure was off. Those who were trying so efficiently to cure me seemed to me at that moment to be trying to put me back under the old tyranny or pressure, and the thought of it nearly broke my heart. That first week in the Manchester hospital was and always will be the lowest ebb of my life.

The hospital doctors took some time deciding what exactly was wrong with me. The final diagnosis I am now given is that mine is a recurrent affective disorder, whereby severe stress can activate an inherited weakness. One of my grandmothers spent the second half of her life in deep mourning, convinced she was condemned to hell for all eternity. To my sister, who was a confidante of hers, she used to say 'My sins, child, are not the sins of commission; they are the sins of omission'. Grandma was so paralysed by the thoughts of how little she had done to deserve heaven, that she ended up doing even less, unable to go out of the house or meet any but a few people, herself always dressed in black. Poor lady, today she could have been cured, and in any case I am quite sure she is in heaven, worthy or unworthy.

After three months or so of the Manchester hospital, the consultant psychiatrist there asked me if I would consent to being given a course of insulin treatment. Since my father was, and my sister is, a doctor I was naturally inclined to trust the consultant, in spite of the rough ride I had been given so far. He told me that the treatment I had been given until then would probably have only a temporary success, as had the same treatment given to me in Oxford, but the insulin treatment, which could only be given to young people, might last me a lifetime. So I gave my consent.

3·'WANDERING LIKE A LOST SHEEP'

During all those four years, spent one in London and three at Heythrop in the country, my heart was still confined in the realms of the Old Testament, as it had been during my noviceship. Although I knew for certain that Jesus was alive and was with me, I was also convinced God's love was conditional. God would love me if I came back to him, but what if, as seemed to be the case, I could not find the way back? Nehemiah tells us he prayed to Yahweh: 'Remember, I beg you, the charge you gave to Moses your servant: "If you prove faithless, I will scatter you . . .; but if you come back to me and keep my commandments and practise them, I would gather [you] back . . ." O Lord, let your ear be attentive to your servant' (cf. Nehemiah 1:8–11). But what was this poor servant to do, who found himself first proved faithless and then unable to return by keeping the rules and requirements the Master seemed to want?

All this, I now see, was only the result of what St Paul calls 'the spirit of a slave' (cf. Romans 8:15) at work in me. If, like the third servant in Jesus' parable of the talents, we are saying to God all the time 'I know you are a hard taskmaster, expecting the last ounce of service out of us your slaves' (cf. Matthew 25.24), then we are inevitably heading for a breakdown of some sort or other. Perhaps we try to keep God's rules to perfection — yes, but why? If all the time we are just trying to keep ahead in the race for heaven, amassing piles of gleaming bricks for our mansion in heaven, then we are liable to snap under the strain or else to look down with a certain smugness on the rest of humanity. If on the other hand we cannot keep up with the race to be perfect, we may find ourselves hiding our failings under a façade of righteousness which is all the more pernicious in that it leads people who are watching us to think that true perfection is not for the likes of themselves. For another reaction to being unable to keep up is to fall back into despair — which is only another face of competition, the face of those for whom the race matters eternally, but it is already lost. All these evils can and do come of believing God to be a hard taskmaster, a measurer of merits. Through no merits of my own I do not think I ever despaired in my cynicism: I simply could not see the way out.

Being under the influence of this spirit of slavery, I naturally put the worst possible interpretation on the Scripture passages that I read in the years of philosophy. Wherever I turned, in the Old Testament or the New, there seemed to be threats pointing at me. When Jesus praises the centurion who 'has soldiers under him, and he says to one man: Go, and he goes; to another: Come here, and he comes; to his servant: Do this, and he does it' (cf. Matthew 8:5ff.), I would immediately think what an unworthy servant I was, worthy of disdain and not praise. The thought that this inability of mine to obey was having an effect on the way I would be for all eternity, that my own precious shining was being dimmed for ever day by day, was well-nigh unbearable.

When in Jesus' parable the doorkeeper is told to be on the watch, I would identify with the doorkeeper, and feel I had given up regular watch-keeping (cf. Mark 13:34). As a student for the priesthood, such a responsible position, I would reckon that my punishment must be all the greater than if I had never answered my vocation at all — but why then had God called me (cf. Luke 12:47f.)? Like Peter, I was a doorkeeper of some sort, with keys of some kind, and I was letting Jesus down. I felt like the steward Shebna with the threat hanging over him: 'I dismiss you from your office, I remove you from your post, and the same day I call on my [other] servant. . . . I invest him with your robe, gird him with your sash, entrust him with your authority; and he shall be a father to the inhabitants of Jerusalem and to the House of Judah. I place the key of the House of David on his shoulder . . .' (cf. Isaiah 22:19–22).

At any hearing of the parable of the talents (Matthew 25:14–30) or the parable of the pounds (Luke 19:11–27), I felt uncomfortably like the wicked servant who buried his talent or wrapped up and hid his one pound: but what else could I do, what with all I had been taught about God and hell, such an exacting Master he must be? And what about the story of the king dividing the sheep from the goats at the final judgement (Matthew 25:31–46)? How much feeding of the hungry had I ever done, how much visiting of the sick or visiting the imprisoned? Even the feeding of minds and hearts which Jesus did first, before feeding the bodies of his listeners (cf. Mark 6:34ff.) — what kind of crumbs had I managed to acquire so far to feed the many who would one day look to me? Four years! Many a teacher was launched into a school with less time of preparation than that, and yet how little I had learnt that could be of any help to anyone else. According to Jesus, 'the workman deserves his keep' (Matthew 10:10); only I seemed no longer to deserve the name of workman.

There seemed to be nothing for it but to admit to God, 'You have repudiated the covenant with your servant and flung his crown dishonoured to the ground' (Psalm 89:39). What *was* the nature of this strange God, whose anger was so quick to blaze (cf. Psalm 2:11f.)? How could he be both a Father and a loving shepherd and yet so swift to anger, terrible anger that could last forever? Perhaps there is only one road, with a false face of God at one end and the loving, true face at the other end of the road? But I could not find in myself the courage or the authority to turn round where I stood and direct my gaze *only* on the loving face of God. I must have been like Francis Thompson in his poem *The Hound of Heaven*, running from the very One he was looking for; or like a lost sheep struggling in a thick hedge or a sharp fence to get away from the hands it did not recognize as those of the shepherd (cf. Luke 15:4); or like Beauty in the fairy-tale, afraid of the Beast because her eyes were blinded to his love, her ears deaf to the tender meaning of his gruff voice. I could understand the reluctance of the invited guests to go to the marriage feast of the king's son, given the king's well-known inclination to terrible vengeance (cf. Matthew 22:1–7). I began to go to pieces, like the man with the unclean spirit who lived among the tombs, and whose heart was pulled a thousand different ways at once (cf. Mark 5:1–9).

But I was still sure there must be an answer somewhere, and I was still praying to have only one way to follow, not a legion, to have my ears opened and the blinds drawn from my eyes, so that I would see and hear and then know what to preach (cf. Mark 7:31–37; 8:22–26). I finally reached that last verse of the longest psalm: 'I am wandering like a lost sheep: come and look for your servant' (Psalm 119:176).

And quite suddenly I was free, free as a bird that escapes from the fowler's net (cf. Psalm 124:6f.). But not for long: in a few weeks I was unable to cope with the new freedom and I found myself once more being pursued by hands that I feared wanted only to clip my wings. Then finally I trusted, and let myself be healed. Though I did not yet hear clearly, the words of the *Hound of Heaven* were spoken also to me:

> 'All which thy child's mistake
> Fancies as lost, I have stored for thee at home:
> Rise, clasp My hand, and come!'

4·TIMES OF CRISIS AND SEEMING DISASTER

Most people, thank God, get through life without a nervous breakdown. But this third stage of my life represents a crisis which everyone has to pass through at some time of their life, since it means a transfer from reliance upon self to reliance on God. The catalyst is usually some event or series of events in our lives, when everything that was going smoothly begins to go wrong. The immediate example that comes to my mind, since it parallels my own life, is that of a student who goes to college or university all full of bright ideals about a future career, only to find that the course seems to have nothing to do with anything. More frequently still, a graduate leaves university contented, only to find many colleagues in the profession seem to have no ideals or the wrong ideals, compared with the dreams of college days. A job or a profession may turn out to have endless rules and regulations, and be run by people who seemingly love rules and regulations above the good of their customers or clients. Those with no job since leaving school or unable to find a job while still young and vigorous feel within themselves that they are appointed by God as 'stewards of creation', yet nobody will give them a share in the work. They can see themselves ending their days having 'done nothing', and if they believe in heaven they may see themselves as being there on sufferance eternally branded as jobless. Married people may be well-nigh shattered by a sudden bereavement or by their marriage going wrong — and so on.

Mercifully, most people's crises are spread out over their lives, and do not come all at once. Whichever of them, as we look back, feels to have been the most dreadful may be the one that taught us most, and taught us to trust God. To take a couple of lofty examples, we might think of Beethoven's deafness or Rembrandt's inability to afford models for his painting because his work was unfashionable. Deafness must have been a terrible blow to Beethoven: I have read somewhere that the famous Funeral March in the 'Eroica' Symphony is originally a funeral march for his own lost hearing. Yet he almost immediately comes out fighting again and writes more wonderful music still and for

42

years to come. Rembrandt bereft of models painted incredibly rich self-portraits of himself as himself or of himself dressed in different costumes. In our lives we too can be shattered but find the truth within ourselves, and then be able to come back, not having to work by formal rules any more but going by instinct, that 'homing instinct' I described earlier.

It is only when we think we have nothing left, that we discover resources in ourselves that we knew nothing about. Before the Good News of God's 'love-with-no-strings' can fully dawn on us, each of us has to learn by bitter experience that our own mind and heart, our will and our hands, are inadequate for God's work. Francis Thompson makes the Voice say in *The Hound of Heaven*:

> All which I took from thee I did but take,
>   Not for thy harms,
> But just that thou might'st seek it in My arms.

God, having shown us our own weakness and taken away all our strength, gives back to us strength of a totally different quality from that which we lost.

But in the meantime these crises and seeming disasters can send us to pieces. A Roman legion had several thousand troops, and the poor crazed man in the gospel was perhaps pulled a thousand ways before the spirit of Jesus calmed him, unified him, integrated his personality. Most of us, too, have felt in ourselves an inability to keep up with our own ideals or ambitions for ourselves, which is in reality an inability to keep up with Jesus unless he gives us his Spirit. Many people know the feeling of stepping ponderously downhill beneath an overhanging cliff when they ought to be climbing upwards: whenever I have suggested in a sermon or a talk that there are periods in our lives when the only way up leads down first, there were nods of recognition and agreement among the hearers. I have never known total despair, but those who have must know it as the total paralysis of all their power for doing good.

The spirit of competition is a snare for many people as it was for me. We can be tempted either to forge ahead and ignore or trample on other people's feelings; we can fall behind in the rat race but still try to keep up appearances; or we can become unduly depressed at having failed in our own eyes and in those of our competitors. Young people can look at the sorry state of the world and vow that their generation is going to put all the world's wrongs right; but then the years go by and there seems to be more, not less, that needs healing. 'In love you created us, in justice you condemned us. . . .' In terms of our idea of justice God cannot but condemn us, and that would have been the end of the story for us all, had not Jesus shown that in God justice is not what we call justice but is forgiveness, endless and fathomless forgiveness. The Good Shepherd does not beat the lost lamb when he finds it, nor even make it walk home: he picks it up on his shoulders, and carries it home rejoicing.

IV
Breakthrough

1·CLIMBING AGAIN

Just a few more steps down, and I was walking on the level. A few paces more again and the path led me round a corner of the cliff to my left, and suddenly everything about the afternoon was changed. I could see now that the path climbed clear up the side of the Rock to what looked to be the summit a thousand feet above. Now this was the real thing, just as I had imagined it!

From now on there could be no more steps leading down; I would be leaning in towards the steps ahead instead of seeming to step out into nothingness. Another look at the path hundreds of feet above me, beckoning me on, and I took a deep breath and started to climb. From here onwards there seemed to be no hurry any more, instead plenty of time to stop and look around. The horizon, which had seemed to close in as I climbed down the steps with the cliff looming to one side, now widened out and I could once again take in the blueness of the Mediterranean, the variety of the moored ships, the fishing boats and pleasure yachts, and the wheeling of the seagulls above and below me. As I climbed again I was surprised and delighted by the wealth of vegetation and the beauty of the wild flowers.

By now it was obvious why the path had been forced to lead me downhill for a time: this was like a valley between sheer cliffs and the path had had to get past that cliff in order to reach this place where it could climb again. My faith was restored in what I had been told about the path, because this was obviously the right path and the one and only path. I wondered why I had ever doubted what I had been told. Now that I was once again eye to eye with the steps ahead, it was clear too that they were in good repair. A whole team of engineers must have put in a lot of hard work, mixing concrete to strengthen steps and erecting safety barriers at tight corners. How they got the heavy materials to such an inaccessible corner of the world was a mystery, and I was grateful.

2·TEACHING, THEOLOGY, ORDINATION, TERTIANSHIP

For the course of insulin treatment in Manchester I was joined by two other young men, one of whom was to become a clergyman in the Church of England, the other a doctor. We were given special beds like fortified cots, because once injected and in our early sleep we tossed and turned, as we fought against the insulin. Then we sweated as the doses increased and the sugar slowly left our blood stream. Then came a long deep sleep, then a coma, and after a half hour or so the watchful male nurses would dose us with glucose to stop the coma from turning into death. By the time it was all over, morning had come, and as we awoke we were given orange juice full of sugar, which was the most beautiful drink I will ever taste, and then a breakfast starting with cornflakes covered with milk and spoonfuls of sugar, which was the most beautiful cereal I will ever taste.

I do not know what the other two dreamed of, but I do remember one dream of mine — indeed I shall never forget it. We had this treatment many times over, and one night in the coma I dreamt that I was already dead. I was in total blackness, yet I could see myself as I climbed without effort up a hill to face my final judgement. With me it was not a case of my whole life being open before my eyes, but I was deeply conscious of the weight of all my scruples: had my sins been confessed? all of them? properly? What about the things I had never confessed but perhaps ought to have confessed? There was no stopping my climb up the hill, however. It struck me as surprising that there was nobody else watching, not even when I reached the top: I had expected to be in full view of everybody. However there was nobody at the top, but only Jesus. I could not see his face clearly, only the general outline of his head and the fact that he was facing me, and his outstretched arms. And what did Jesus do? Did he accuse, or question me? What did he say? He said nothing, he simply took me in his arms and gave one enormous hug, a hug that somehow said without a single word: 'Gerald, why were you afraid?! You were you, and I was who I am, and I have been with you all down your days till now, closer to you than you are to yourself, loving

46

you.' That hug or embrace, I can feel it still, went to the marrow of my bones and the heart of my heart. Strange, I suppose, that I should see myself climbing the hill, as if from the outside, but that I should be at one with myself when face to face with Jesus and embraced by his arms. And that was all, until I woke up to that unspeakably delicious orange juice.

Now whether this dream was real, more real than ordinary vision, or whether it was 'just a dream', I cannot say. All I can say is that from that day onwards I have never been troubled by scruples again, or by any fear of hell. For myself, I am sure meeting with Jesus is like that, and he is just the same now and will be just the same whenever I meet him face to face. Within myself, I am sure he is like that not just for me but for anyone else at all. How could he have two faces, one for me and one for someone else?

Some years later I came across John Blackburn's description of insulin treatment as seen by a male nurse, who watched over the cots and gave the injections of insulin (the treatment is not in use any more). To my surprise and pleasure, he wrote in his book *A Sour Apple Tree* (Secker and Warburg, London 1958) of the uncanny feeling he and his nursing colleagues had, not only that the patients were dreaming of, and sorting out, their past deep anxieties, but also that they were doing it in some other mysterious world.

After a certain period of convalescence in the hospital itself and a longer spell at home with my parents, the question was raised, did I want to go back to the Jesuits at all, or to call it a day and take up some other kind of life instead? In spite of everything, I wanted to go back. If the truth be known, I could not bear to give up the daily hour or thereabouts of prayer with God, even though my prayer-time was usually pretty much of a blank. The Father Provincial and his advisers considered it would be unwise for me to go as originally planned to Campion Hall in Oxford to read classics. What I needed was a busy life, but one not involving further study for the present. So I was appointed to St John's, a Jesuit preparatory school — that is, a private boarding school for boys aged from 8 to 13 or 14 — near Windsor, and my parents drove me down, a leisurely journey by way of the Wye Valley and Bath and Salisbury Cathedral and Stonehenge, none of which I had ever seen before. I joined the staff at St John's in September 1958, at the age of twenty-four.

Life with small boys turned out to be just the very thing to bring me back to normal. It is hard to be over-serious for long with such lively companions. The headmaster and staff were most welcoming, and to begin with I had only about fifteen lessons a week to teach, but quite a lot of supervision duty during the boys' study or free time. My first sign of returning life appeared when the question came up, who was to produce the annual play at the end of November. I volunteered, and decided to put on just the Pyramus and Thisbe sections of *A Midsummer Night's Dream*: the forming of the project, the rehearsal in the forest and the play itself, without the nuisance of the supercilious onlookers of the original play. The six lads were magnificent, perfect for their parts, and the little show was funnier than most I have seen, amateur or professional. I came to life yet again during the following Lent, when with a much bigger cast we put on a beautiful Passion play, in the school chapel. I should say, Passion *mime*: young amateur actors can be much more expressive if they have no lines to speak, so we had them mime their parts to someone else's reading of the gospel story. Even we who had devised the mime found ourselves with tears in our eyes as we watched the final presentation.

Still sometimes at night I would cry tears of perplexity for myself: going through a mental hospital as a patient is like going through a hurricane in a small boat, and recovery does not come suddenly. But my second year at St John's was much more 'back to normal' than the first. I taught a pretty full timetable of lessons, I was form teacher to my own class of ten-year-olds, I was still doing a lot of supervision, I did my best with such refereeing and umpiring of games as came my way, and was acting Scoutmaster for that year. The school has a beautiful outdoor pool and that summer term was one in which the British weather excelled itself; in May a film company borrowed the pool and heated it lest the leading lady catch cold, so we were able to swim every day from May to mid-October, in very warm water as well as sunshine.

As a keeper of discipline I was quite good outside the classroom, average inside it. At another school a dozen years later, where corporal punishment was rarely if ever used, I managed to survive the year's teaching without resorting to such drastic methods, but here at St John's I had to rely on it too often for my liking. I can only hope and pray the recipients will forgive me. However, it was mainly in the classroom; in the dormitory there was never any bother, which was a relief to one who has always liked his beauty sleep. One of the surprises I received in the class-room was the discovery that I no longer believed in the popular version of the ten plagues and the Exodus, but what to believe instead was unclear to me. In general as a teacher I followed the principle of picking out what was the next step each pupil needed to learn, and correcting that carefully, overlooking much else that might be wrong. Nothing is more depressing for a learner than to get back an exercise covered with the teacher's red ink, but anyone can cope with just one step forward. For English essays with my own class I would sometimes let them choose their own favourite subject and tell them they could write as much as they liked and I would read but not correct it: they in turn must be prepared to read it out to the rest of the class. I got some lovely stories, including one fence-by-fence account of how the writer rode the winner in the Grand National Steeplechase at Aintree! I enjoyed being a form-teacher.

Since the end of the novitiate I had been playing the piano again, but here at St John's I finally gave it up and bought a guitar instead. Practising the piano during term-time was impossible, because at the only times when I was free there were boys within earshot of the piano, either at study or in bed sleeping. During vacations I could get back to the standard I had reached the previous vacation, but never make any progress; so I took to the Spanish guitar whose sound had always thrilled me. If the Psalmist could say, 'with the harp I will solve my problem', then perhaps with the guitar I could solve a few of mine. One problem was solved right away: I could practise quietly every day now. By the end of the school year I was already able to accompany most of the songs we sang at the Scout camp-fires. Another new experience I had always had a yearning for was sailing, and my first chance of this came in one of the summer holiday fortnights spent with other Jesuits, this time at Brixham in Devon. Two sepa-rate benefactors had kindly given us the use of a sailing dinghy and an off-shore sailing cruiser, and I had my first lessons in handling a boat at sea. Besides being a joy themselves, these days at sea gave me a lot of understanding of the principles of spiritual discernment — 'spirit' and 'wind' being at root the same word.

In 1960, after two years at St John's, I was asked to move up to the senior school, Beaumont College, for a further year of teach-ing. I must confess I did not enjoy life as much at Beaumont as I had at St John's; a teacher needs a longer, not a shorter, time to settle in and become part of a senior school. I am sure I would have felt more at home given another year or two, but by then it was time to move to the study of theology. From my year at Beaumont my most vivid memories are of the Queen's visit to the school — it was the centenary year — and of the centenary play I produced with the younger boys of the college: *The Birds* of Aristophanes, in a modern English translation (with additions and subtractions to suit the occasion). We did the play out of doors, using a stage on the lawn in front of the balcony of the beautiful old college building, the 'White House'. The mortals inhabited the stage, the birds the balcony, and the visiting goddess was let down by a winch from an upper storey window. The play is about getting relations right between mortals and the gods, and is great fun. The happy memory is clouded only by one thought: I had no contingency plans should it rain on the evenings of the play! Fortunately, the evenings were fine if chilly; but I would never take such a chance again. It would have been grossly unfair to let all that hard work of the many, many actors go for nothing. Probably in the event of disaster we would have moved into the big indoor hall and done the best we could.

Next, following the year at Beaumont, came the four years' study of theology. Arrangements were made with the Irish Province of the Jesuits for me to go to Milltown Park in Dublin for the four years instead of back to Heythrop; I think the authorities at Heythrop did not fancy my coming back there to break down again. So after a holiday with my parents I sailed on the B&I daytime ferry from Liverpool to Dublin in September 1961.

That journey across the sea, seeing one land fade into the horizon astern and a new land growing clearer ahead brought a very cleansing feeling to my mind and heart. The sun was shining, all the fears and terrors of my 'slavery' were gone, I had grown back to my former health and strength, and ahead lay the last main period of study, which promised to be real, whereas for me the study of philosophy had been like chasing shadows. The dream which had marked my change of heart had been of Jesus, not the Father, but I experienced it as true, an assurance given with all the authority of the Father. Little by little it was beginning to dawn on me that the Father's love is equally like an all-forgiving embrace, and that if one faces the loving Father fairly and squarely, everything else falls into perspective. He has not two faces, only the one loving face: it is we human beings who can face two ways. What turns us away from God is fear, fear of ourselves really. Only Jesus has the power to turn us around again. From now on I could serve God without fear of failure, because I had hit rock bottom and *still* Jesus accepted me without question. There was nothing further to fear. A well was beginning to bubble up in my heart, saying all the time 'The Father loves you; the Father loves you', so I was coming to be like an ancient city with its own fresh water supply within the city walls.

The four-year course in theology lived up to all my expectations, and more. The first course to catch my interest deeply introduced us to what modern science and criticism had discovered about the Scriptures, their history and meaning. Almost immediately I decided to divide up the New Testament into four parts, one part to each year, and pray my way through it during each morning's hour of meditation, using a good modern commentary. In my first year I prayed through Mark's gospel and the letters of Peter, and Mark has remained my favourite gospel. In fact, during the four years of theology I wrote a long rambling book on Mark's gospel, nearly six hundred pages in length, which fortunately for the general reading public was never published. But I still cherish and use many of the ideas and themes which came to me as I wrote. Later I made two attempts at revising and shortening the book, but finally shelved it.

The course on the Church was interesting. Father James Corboy, the lecturer, surprised us by saying the First Vatican Council had left unfinished business and the proposed new Council would probably balance papal infallibility by some kind of collegiality among the bishops. A year or two later he was made a bishop himself and became one of the Council Fathers. The course in moral theology, training us to hear confessions and give counsel, was from a priest much gentler, warmer and more enlightened than the textbook he was expected to teach from. Our copies ended up with page after page crossed out on his instructions and his own kindly notes written in. But all the lecturers were good, not just the ones who gave us those three courses.

On our days off I usually went climbing up the hills with a Jesuit companion, or into the city, or to visit friends, relations and benefactors who lived near enough to Milltown. There were several individuals and families who opened their doors and made me welcome. I discovered I had a talent for telling stories to children, and must have spent hours giving them my version of tales from *The Arabian Nights* and any other good stories I could find. By this time I could also entertain children and others with songs to my own guitar accompaniment, and I would never get nervous about these performances as I used to when playing the piano for people.

On the feast of St Ignatius Loyola, 1964, I was ordained priest, after three of the four years of theology. There were no problems about no family being present this time: my own family and closest relations came to the ceremony, and over fifty friends and relations to the Mass the following day, at which I was the sole celebrant for the first time. During communion time at Mass and at the reception afterwards I was puzzled and perplexed about something I could not share with anyone till a long time afterwards: this was, that I had a horrible feeling the whole of my Mass was make-believe and not faith. In fact, I later realized, it was a matter of faith: till that moment I had always had a presumption that whereas I and all other lay people *believed* in the presence of Christ in the Eucharist, a priest could *see*; now here was I a priest and I could see no better than before. There is a kind of parallel in the way couples after their wedding ceremony often do not feel married, because they expect to feel different but they feel just the same as before.

The fourth year of theology followed, and most mornings we newly-ordained students would go out to say Mass for religious communities around the city; most weekends we would stay at one of Dublin's many churches, helping with confessions on Saturday and saying one or two of the Sunday morning masses. All in all I stayed at thirty-seven different churches that year, and I must have heard thousands of confessions. In some of the big new churches in recently-built housing estates, I found it surprisingly easy to preach a homily to 2,000 people at a time. The confessions I never found too many, doing my best to show to others the kindness Jesus had shown me.

Now at last I felt like a servant of God again, but without any trace of competition any more. Somehow in the past being a good servant had come to eclipse being God's son in my heart; now since the breakdown I knew once and for all that God loves me not because I am his servant but because I am his son, and not because I am a good son but because I am *his* son. Relying now solely on his love for me as his own son, I tried to thank him as a good son should by a life of faithful service, but knowing I was already forgiven if I should fail once more. The servant was a servant again, but the terms of employment were entirely different. As with the prodigal son, there had been in my life a time of son-ship, then a time of independence chasing goals not required by my Father, a time of destitution, a deep renewed consciousness of my Father's generosity, and a subsequent desire to serve him — to serve *him*, not my own previous distorted image of him.

From studies in St Mark's gospel and the first letter of St Peter I had come to know Jesus as the Servant of his Father and of all mankind in his death. What I had gone through in the two breakdowns did not now strike me as having been my cross, so much as Jesus' cross impinging on my life. It was as if Jesus had stood by me in the very lowest ebb of my life, and said to the whole world, 'See, one of the least of my little ones; he comes with me', and the world had crucified him for daring to wait for me. If he really was the Son of God, he would know better than to wait for the likes of me, the world would say. Jesus was my servant because, knowing his Father's mind, he waited behind for me whatever the cost to himself.

From Ireland I came back in the summer of 1965 across the Irish Sea to St Beuno's in North Wales for the year of tertianship. The tertianship is in some ways like a third year of novitiate, with once again the full *Spiritual Exercises* of St Ignatius. This was followed by some study of the *Constitutions* which St Ignatius formulated for the organization and running of the Society of Jesus and the preparation of its members for their work in the world, and then several controlled experiments in giving retreats. There was a fair amount of peace and quiet during the year, so I spent a lot of time reading right through the Old Testament with the best guidebook in the library.

There was just one main reflection that came to me after the long retreat of the *Exercises*, and it was this: whereas in the first time of praying the Passion of Christ in the course of the *Exercises* as a novice I had always imagined myself standing watching Jesus up there on his cross, now in this second time through the *Exercises* I had found myself up there on the cross, looking down, Jesus and me together. I did not plan it that way; it simply happened, and I noticed the difference only some time afterwards. Once I had made this observation it became easier to become reconciled to the fact that Jesus had for some time been harder to picture in my imagination at prayer than in the early days of religious life: if he was within me looking out, listening with my ears, reaching with my hands, then no wonder I could not see him clearly any more. He must be too close, not too far. I suspect that the moment when the change occurred was the final moment of my coma dream, but it was now, eight years later, that I pieced together that particular puzzle. Jesus had died to save me; now in me and with me he wanted to live and die for others.

But if Jesus uses my feet to go where he wills, then I am not standing beside him any more, I am standing where he stands. So it comes about that the Father's love comes straight to where I am, and the 'Abba! Father!' I pray to him rises to him in the voice of Jesus. The journey into God has taken a new turn.

3·'ABBA! FATHER!'

I entitled this section of my life 'Breakthrough', not meaning that I broke through to anything, but that Jesus broke through to me. So the first Scripture passages that come to mind are of Jesus waking up in the boat, of the shepherd finding the lost sheep, of Jesus appearing to the two disciples on the road to Emmaus, of Jesus breaking through into the life of St Paul.

Jesus was asleep in the boat while it was nearly swamped; the disciples were very much afraid, and woke him up. Jesus stilled the storm and said 'Why are you so frightened? How is it that you have no faith?' (cf. Mark 4:38–40)

The shepherd took the lost sheep on his shoulders and joyfully carried it home (cf. Luke 15:5). I once saw a picture on a calendar, a photograph of a Yorkshire shepherd sitting in the front parlour of the inn of which he was also the landlord. He sat on a wooden chair with a pint of beer in his hand, in front of a fire blazing in an old fashioned grate. His shepherd's crook was propped up against the wall. Lying asleep on a newspaper in front of the hearth, looking the picture of contentment, was a new-born lamb; beside the shepherd's feet and keeping warm before the fire was a bowl containing a baby's milk bottle, half full. That picture reminded me strongly of the days and months when I was coming round after the ordeal of illness and hospital.

Seeing Jesus in the coma dream was to me like the experience of the two disciples on the road to Emmaus and at Emmaus (cf. Luke 24:13–35). They had too gambled their whole lives on Jesus, only to lose him. Now here he was again, and from now on no one could ever take him away from them. Jesus must also have taught them about the Servant songs in the Scriptures, since he spoke to them at length about how it was ordained that the Christ should suffer and so enter into his glory (cf. v. 26).

St Paul's conversion seems almost to have taken his breath away for a time: he did not launch straight into a lengthy career as an apostle; he soon found he needed some years away by himself to rethink his theology in the light of his encounter with Jesus (cf. Galatians 1:17).

For me the breakdown and breakthrough were like an Exodus: 'When Israel was a child I loved him, and I called my son out of Egypt. . . . I myself taught Ephraim to walk, I took them in my arms. . . . I led them with reins of kindness, with leading-strings of love' (cf. Hosea 11:1, 3–4). I would never again be a slave to a false image of God. Although my dream was of Jesus, it led me to turn my eyes more and more to my Father. Where Jesus says 'Anyone who does the will of God, that person is my brother and sister and mother', I understood now that the will of God is to be my Father (cf. Mark 3:35). To do the will of God is to let him be my Father. That must be his first wish. His second wish is surely that I try to be as forgiving to all others as he has already been to me. The king had forgiven me all my debt of ten thousand talents, had forgiven me when I was resisting him, when I was running away from him (cf. Ephesians 2:4f.); now he certainly wished me to forgive those who owned me a small sum like five hundred denarii (cf. Matthew 18:23–35). In restoring me as his son and removing all my fears, for the past and for the future, my Father had given me a pearl beyond price, without asking any return. Therefore I wanted to give him what return I could, by giving unconditional forgiveness to all who ever hurt me. If I believed in the forgiveness of sins, I wanted to believe in forgiving others as I had been forgiven myself. God is the forgiveness of sins, not just my sins.

In the parable of the labourers in the vineyard (Matthew 20: 1–16), I now noticed how those who came to work at the eleventh hour received the same wage from the generous owner of the vineyard as those who had laboured all day, and that to myself I only seemed to have started working for God, the real God, since my breakdown. As I hoped my fellow human beings would be generous with me and not complain to God about my late arrival, so I would try to be generous with those who did complain, and with those who after me might perhaps not arrive till the eleventh hour and beyond.

Like St Paul, I needed some time 'in the desert' to look at the world from the entirely new perspective Jesus had given me. As Hosea had planned for his unfaithful wife and as God had planned for faithless people, so he had planned for me, 'to lure and lead me out into the wilderness and speak to my heart: there I would respond to him as I did when I was young' (cf. Hosea 2:16f.).

The motive for serving God now — serving my Father with and in Jesus — was coming to be love and gratitude rather than anything else. With the Psalmist I asked myself, 'What return can I make to Yahweh for all his goodness to me?'; and the answer was there, 'I shall take up the cup of salvation, and call on the name of Yahweh' (cf. Psalm 116:12f.). In Christian terms, taking the cup meant accepting the future along with Jesus, determined never to doubt God's love and forgiveness again, no matter what might happen. With the prodigal son, I was starting to make my way back to my Father's house, planning all the while how I could be of service to him in thanks for his simply being there, utterly reliable in his love for me his unworthy son. Unworthy son? Yes surely: I had been calling a false image of God 'Father' for long enough.

'The son of Man himself did not come to be served but to serve, and to give his life as a ransom for many' (Mark 10:45). He did not come to glory in being the divine Son of God, but to redeem us as adopted sons and daughters of God. Giving his life as a ransom for me meant losing all his glory for a time: 'His state was divine, yet he did not cling to his equality with God but emptied himself to assume the condition of a slave, and became as men are' (Philippians 2:6–7a). True to his own principles, Jesus chose the lowest place at the banquet (Luke 14:7–11) so as to sit beside the most neglected guests of all, and take them to the top places as sons or daughters. At long last my own desire to be friend to all the world slipped into place as part of my vocation to be a servant of God. Jesus was my servant in that he who is the truth offered me friendship when I was completely shattered: he need not have bothered to stand up for the mentally shattered and broken-hearted, but he did stand up for them. So from now on my service of God would continue to include the desire to be warm and friendly to all, especially the most neglected. Jesus seems to deflect thanks from himself, and instead turns the attention of those he has healed towards his Father, to thank the Father instead (cf. Luke 17:11–19, the story of the ten lepers).

One thing is certain, with the coma dream I moved once and for all into the New Testament and away from the Old. Now I knew that God's love is unconditional. He loves the helpless and the sinners (cf. Romans 5:6, 10), those frozen in inactivity and those running away from him, as much as he loves those who have never deserted him. For the children of the king there are no taxes (cf. Matthew 17:24–27), no demands without whose fulfilment God will not love us. When we keep rules, even God's rules, we do not now keep them in order to secure God's love, which is ours already, but as a free offering.

Now at the end of my long years of training, and about to be sent out as an apostle, I was aware that God had entrusted to us young apostles the news that the men and women of the whole world are already reconciled to him and we were ambassadors for Christ (cf. 2 Corinthians 5:19–20).

4·COMING TO TERMS WITH REALITY

From my observation of other people's lives, I would suspect that many, if not most, go though some kind of crisis in early adult life, to come out of it wiser and happier. Looking around for a metaphor to describe what I mean, I am reminded of a runner who sets out breathing well, then finds breathing unbearably painful, but before long comes through to what we call a 'second wind', an easier form of breathing which feels like an unexpected gift. St Thérèse of Lisieux compared herself to a toddler unable to climb the stairs till her Father comes down and picks her up. St Teresa of Avila wrote that by God's gift we may move from a noisy man-made set of cisterns, buckets and pipes to give us our water, to an almost silent well. What is happening in ourselves, without metaphors, is that we come to terms with reality; we find we can keep our ideals without compromising, without being restricted or overawed by other people. Somehow we come through our crisis with our ideals now attainable, in a manner we could never have planned for ourselves. A student moves from one subject to another more congenial; a young man manages to find a job that suits him better; a woman finds an enriching way of spending her days in unemployment instead of pining over her situation. Many simply carry on from where they were before, but now they know how to pace themselves better. A marriage partner may be the God-given means of someone's learning to move at a pace that can go on for ever.

Obviously shifts of mind and heart like these can and should happen without a breakdown and hospital. And nobody need feel bereft at never having had a dream such as that one which came to me in one of my comas — a coma is nearer to death than most people would care to go before their time. But, if my assurance may count for anything, I did not experience the dream as being for myself alone — as I said, if Jesus is like that for me, he is like that for anybody and everybody. His divine reassurance may be like a rock hidden in our lives beneath layers of sand and earth and clay, but in times of crisis we come closer to where he is, and he is always ready to support us. We even talk about 'reaching rock bottom' in times of crisis. We reach the rock, or as near to it as Providence lets us go for now; and then once again we begin to build our lives, but on a entirely different foundation from before.

People coming out of a crisis like this may sometimes be scornful of what they have left behind, laughing at the rules and regulations of their former restricted life. Perhaps they have to react like this to prove to themselves that they are free. A kinder way of proceeding was that of Jesus when he told Peter to pay the Temple tax for the two of them, 'so as not to offend these people', the collectors. St Paul, too, asked those with freer consciences not to scandalize the others who were still scrupulous about eating food that had earlier been offered to idols. Jesus himself was scathing in his attacks on the scribes and Pharisees who tied people up with regulations, but Jesus was not newly emerging from enslavement himself; he was speaking with full spiritual maturity. For the rest of us it is usually better to digest fully the Good News for ourselves, before we decide who the real enemy is. In the meantime, 'Do not judge, and you will not be judged yourselves' is still a safe and wonderful guide.

The Good News is that I can, from anywhere at all, call God 'my Father, my beloved Father', knowing that his love for me never changes no matter what direction I am facing. We are accustomed as Christians to pray quite frequently to Jesus 'Take my hands, my eyes, my ears, my mouth, my heart and use them as your own', and we need not be surprised if he takes us at our word — but then we can expect not to see him so clearly, because he will be closer to us than we are to ourselves. Instead we shall find our eyes directed more and more to his Father and our Father, and to all the poor of the world who are in danger of being left behind or left out of consideration. But now we work for them with peace in our hearts, since our own place (and theirs) in our Father's heart is assured.

One surprise I received in telling stories to children concerned Hans Andersen's *The Ugly Duckling*. Only then did it come to me that the duckling had been a little swan all along, but nobody had told him till in exile he saw the two swans on the lake; then his heart told him, at long last, this was where he belonged.

V

Crusade

1·THE ZIG-ZAG PATH UPWARD

I was by now growing more confident with every step. The way to the summit was clear all the time. True, I was growing more tired and hotter as the afternoon wore on, but the compensations were correspondingly great, and I was very glad I had come. From half way up the side of the Rock the view was magnificent, not so much of the distant coastline which was shrouded in mist as of the sheer size and scale of the Rock itself. The road by the sea was a thin ribbon, the carpark seemed to be half-filled with beetles but they were cars. Along to the north I could see the vast bare concrete slopes built to catch the winter rains and direct the water into huge storage tanks within the Rock itself. Where I stood was level with half way up these slopes. The seagulls were wheeling well below me; it seemed strange to be watching seagulls from above.

By contrast with the huge Rock, the tiny flowers beside the steps were all the more delicate. Sometimes they nestled in the corners between one step and the next. I stopped to take a picture of some little yellow daisy-like flowers, and then some pale pink flowers like convolvulus with a shape similar to ear-trumpets. There was a city on the other side of the Rock, but here I was alone with the Rock.

The path zig-zagged its way upwards towards the summit. I was somewhat startled to find that there were occasional choices to be made: the path went on straight, and another zig-zagged to left or right and took almost the opposite direction. Which was the one to follow? I did not want to get lost on a hillside that dropped almost sheer below. The first parting of the ways had a rickety signpost, pointing to the change of direction as being the Mediterranean Steps. That was all right: I just hoped that neither wind nor human hand had pushed the pointer round to the wrong direction. The next choice of ways had a post but no pointer on it. I cautiously tried out both ways to see which looked the more promising. One was strewn with debris and soon arrived at a ruined gun-emplacement perched on a cliff, so the other was obviously the one to follow.

The last point of choice was more alarming. The zig-zag alternative, the one which doubled back above the way I had come, was nothing like as wide or well-kept as the way I had followed so far; the other alternative, straight ahead, soon landed me up at the concreted entrance to a cave — beside a cliff, so the cave must be the way ahead? I have never liked caves, and shied away from this one. The zig-zag path must be right after all — and it was. The quality of the path and steps soon improved again, and I carried on climbing.

2·SENT BY THE FATHER: SOLID YEARS OF PREACHING AND TEACHING

Time was, when near the end of the year of tertianship, the young Jesuit priests would simply find a list of names and places on the noticeboard one day, and look down to it see where they were destined for — some of them thus finding out for the first time. This was rather the spirit in which I had been trained for the past fourteen years, so I was no little upset when the Father Provincial came in person to see us, and in my interview asked me what I would like to do next. All well and good, if I had been led to expect such a genial enquiry all along: then I could have had years to build up a special interest in one or another aspect of the ministry, though still being prepared as a good Jesuit to find that some other line was more in demand. My special interest in the last five years had been Scripture, but the Provincial and his advisers did not see a future there for me; so too as regards the degree in classics or English which had been postponed when I broke down, both options seemed to carry too much risk of another breakdown. I had done well to get ordained and finish the training; no need to run unnecessary risks. What about a course in Liturgy — I had a good singing voice and presence on the altar, and the imagination to devise celebrations? In the end, after twenty-four hours there at the crossroads, the decision was for a course in Catechetics and Religious Education, at Lumen Vitae Institute in Brussels, as soon as a place for me could be reserved there. So in the end I got my way (in both senses), since I hardly knew the word catechetics and this was certainly the Provincial's decision, not mine. In the event, as he had foreseen, the scope of work involved in catechetics suited my capabilities and interests very well: for instance, I have been able to study and use the Scriptures in a way much more congenial to me than the exact textual criticism demanded in most courses of pure Scripture.

Thus finally the servant was sent out: as I like to think, sent by the Father, to go with Jesus wherever Jesus is sent. In my heart I go as son of the Father, but desiring to be allowed to be of service along the way home. By now, as I had hoped from the beginning, I was not only being sent out but I knew what to say; indeed the message itself was taking over as the motivation for each step of the way. By now, I knew for certain that Jesus is risen, alive and here — and the most wonderful person that ever walked the earth. I knew he was there like the poor man Lazarus in every person I met, no matter how self-assured they might appear; I knew that Jesus is beside each one, going back to the Father, and that he shares one Spirit or homesickness with the Father, so that when I know Jesus is all-forgiving I know the Father is too. All of this comes out of the gospels, but was not always the usual emphasis in preaching even in 1966, so I had to start matching my message to the people to whom I was sent. I did so with slowly growing confidence, as it became clear that the truths dearest to me were exactly what so many knew they needed to hear. I threw away most of my theology notes, and started again from the things closest to my heart.

In the last few months at St Beuno's we were all sent out to preach our first retreats to students in day schools and boarding schools, to adult laypeople, to religious Sisters and Brothers. The first big reaction I got was in the schools, when I assured the teenage pupils that God loved them no matter what. Whether they were in their own eyes too tall or too short, too thin or too fat, good at games or no good at games . . . and so on. They loved that, and drank it in; they really did.

We had applied too late for me to go to Brussels in 1966, so I was booked in for autumn the following year. In the meantime in September 1966 I was asked by the Provincial to go for a year to Loyola Hall, a Jesuit retreat house near Liverpool. During the year I preached retreats both at the Hall and around and about the whole country. 'Preached' is not however the right word for those of the retreats which were for 16- to 18-year-olds, since the youngsters were expected to co-operate in other ways besides listening: what I mean is that most of the retreats of that year were not 'directed' retreats where retreatants are taken one by one, at their own pace. Even preached retreats do of course allow for private interviews if a retreatant so wishes. I used the guitar a lot in these early days as a priest, mostly as an ice-breaker. Children especially were always delighted to hear a priest singing a folk-song or a popular song, and then they were more inclined to listen when I was offering them a truth that might help them. One place I regularly played was a school within walking distance of Loyola Hall, a small boarding-school for girls run by Sisters, the children coming mostly from unhappy homes. My heart went out to them, and where the prophet Micah had said one of the only three things Yahweh asks of me is 'to love tenderly', I began as if for the first time to understand that a priest need not be afraid of his own heart.

In preaching retreat after retreat to adults, a retreat-giver inevitably repeats himself and begins to notice what are the things he never leaves out. With me it was to take the words of the voice from heaven in the baptism of Jesus, 'You are my Son, the Beloved; my favour rests on you', or as it is in another translation, 'You are my beloved Son; with you I am well pleased', and to invite the listeners to put the words on themselves, try them for size as it were. We too are baptized, so any of us can hear the Father saying to us 'You are my beloved daughter', or 'You are my beloved son, with you I am well pleased'. God does not change his mind, so he is still saying the same thing today, and I can always look at him and say 'I am your beloved child; you are well pleased with me'.

In 1967, after the year of retreat-giving, it was time to go to Lumen Vitae Institute in Brussels for the year of catechetics. I went with one good companion from the British Jesuits, and we both enjoyed the year. There were students (all mature students, laypeople and religious and secular clergy) from thirty-seven different countries, and the mutual welcome and community life at the institute probably taught us even more about catechetics than the lectures. Catechetics has to do with deepening and developing a faith that is already explicit in a person, whereas evangelization is to do with how best to go about helping people find faith within their own lives. Many if not most of us would be going back to work also among people who thought they had experienced faith only to find it wanting. In Brussels as in every other year of my life I found good friends who were kind to me far beyond my deserts ('houses, brothers, sisters, mothers, children and land . . .', as Jesus had promised); in particular I recall the kindness of one English lady living outside Brussels who was dying of cancer, who thought she had lost faith but who gave me far more than a cup of cold water because I was a disciple of Jesus.

Coming back to England in the summer of 1968, I was asked to go back to Loyola Hall at least for the time being. My chief joy in going back was the knowledge that I could pick up the threads of friendship with the children at the school up the hill. This was to be the final year of its existence, but some of the girls have remained firm friends of mine to this day, inviting me to their weddings and the christenings of their children, and other celebrations. Two shocks mark the year for me. First of all, a mole on my cheek turned out to be a malignant melanoma, a little cancer malignant but local — a potential killer. I had been dithering about it until Father Jerome O'Hea, an elderly ex-missioner then on the staff of Loyola Hall, told me to stop dithering and get the thing diagnosed because it might be dangerous. I was whisked into Whiston hospital and the melanoma was thoroughly uprooted, the gap in my cheek being covered over again with skin taken from my chest. The shock was not so much in the brush with death, which was rather exciting, as in the loss of my own face as I had known and (now I knew) loved it as a vital part of my personality. Even when a few years later another surgeon at the same hospital did an equally expert job in removing the skin-graft and remodelling my face, to me it was not the same. St Luke the doctor tells us that once when Jesus cured a possessed man the devil came out of the man 'without hurting him at all', and I now had to believe that Jesus in his own way would give me my own face back. In the meantime I am very grateful to the surgeons, the nurses and — Father Jerome O'Hea.

The other shock was irremediable by science: my sister, my brother and I lost our father, our mother lost her husband. It was all over in a few traumatic days, and he who had cured and cared for thousands of patients had a lonely little death. The funeral tried to make up for the loneliness: I have never seen so many mourners at a funeral of a layman, many of them having been brought into the world by him, many more owing their lives to him. One element in the shock at the death of the first parent to go to heaven is the sudden feeling that now no more is known about heaven and earth than we know in our own minds and hearts. Even though by the time their parents die most children have long ceased to look to them for answers, there still lingers on the deep-rooted feeling that there is someone older and wiser to whom we can turn for reassurance. The shepherd is gone for the time being: now we must take full responsibility for our world and be shepherds ourselves.

In the autumn of 1969 I was sent to Glasgow to set up the Religious Education Centre at the invitation of the Archbishop, Dr Scanlon. This I did, and it has survived, though I myself only survived there for one year. There were differences of opinion (not with His Grace, I may say) as to what was the purpose of having such a Centre, and the Father Provincial withdrew me to make a point. One of the blessings of a religious order such as the Jesuits is that a man may be at the centre of a rumpus in one diocese one day, and working quietly in a different diocese the next — or as soon as he has recovered from being at the centre of the storm, as I did with my sister and her husband. I was happy to observe that within a very few years of my departure all the permissions I had been standing out for were granted to my successors at the Centre. On the lighter and brighter side, I enjoyed Scotland enormously, not least the life at the University Chaplaincy where I lodged, some Saturday walks on the mountains with students and their Jesuit chaplain (who was a rock of support to me in my catechetical struggles), and breezy seaside days-off with a large and lovely family of friends in West Kilbride on the Ayrshire coast.

Back in England in the summer of 1970 I was asked to act for a year as Head of Religious Education in a Catholic school for boys and girls aged eleven to sixteen, in the Liverpool Archdiocese; the school was in the town of Widnes, and its pupils were those who had 'failed' to pass the examination into the selective secondary schools. This two-tier system of secondary education was then in its last few years, before comprehensive schools were introduced. Thus I was very well suited by inclination to work with these youngsters, many of whom already felt they had been left behind by fortune. I found teaching in Widnes far more demanding than the years of teaching in a Jesuit school, not because the pupils were slower on the uptake, they were not, but they were far less well motivated than the pupils at St John's or Beaumont College with their fee-paying parents. Here in Widnes, unless teachers were very strict disciplinarians they had to catch the pupils' interest from the start of the lesson. Occasional days of near desperation drove me to some valuable discoveries: I found that the middle years of the school gave of their best when working each at their own pace on interesting workcards giving them a choice of free composition, answering questions, drawing expressively, writing a poem, on a particular theme. So I spent the Christmas holidays composing sets of such workcards, as colourful and attractive as I could make them. These worked like a charm, and enabled me to move towards my old method of teaching, namely finding out where each pupil stood and encouraging them to take the next step forward.

Among the teaching staff I made some good friends, who also helped me to come to grips with teaching in this situation that was so new to me. The youngsters were kind too, and I was very fond of them. I can see the advantage of staying at a school for some years: in Widnes I got on famously with the first-year pupils and almost as well with the second-year pupils. If I could have still been there when they moved into their third and fourth years we could have bridged the gap that exists between healthily shy (in matters religious) adolescents and their teachers. However, it was not to be: after one year at the school, though I did not move house from St Francis Xavier's parish house where I had lived whilst teaching in Widnes, I did change jobs. I hope the year of teaching gave the boys and girls something of value; to me it gave the invaluable knowledge of how difficult it is to teach religion to a class where some are keen but the majority are indifferent about the subject.

In September 1971 I joined the staff of the Christian Education Centre in Liverpool at the invitation of His Grace Archbishop Beck. Under the English and Welsh system of Catholic education the state provides inspectors and advisers in all subjects except religious education; in all that concerns religion the bishops provide their own inspectorate and advisory services. The Christian Education Centre is such an advisory service for the Archdiocese of Liverpool, and was founded by Father Anthony Bullen who was still the Director when I joined. I had done small items of work for him in my last year at Loyola Hall, and indeed had tried to model the Religious Education Centre in Glasgow on Father Bullen's way of proceeding at Liverpool. Thus at long last I was able to settle in to one task which was to last for ten years. As a careful reader may have noticed, I had in seven years lived in seven different places, and all this restlessness was beginning to do me no good. From now on for ten years there might be changes of emphasis within the work, but there was no more physical uprooting.

Earlier in these pages I wrote that although I see myself as a lieutenant rather than a natural leader of men, there have been some important exceptions. One of these exceptions is a certain doggedness in me which owes nothing to anybody else. As an illustration I recall the one and only physical game at which I excelled at school, a game invented by the physical education teacher and called by him Struggleball. The class was divided into two teams, a large mat was placed at either end of the gymnasium, a big rubber medicine-ball was bounced in between the teams and then it was up to each to struggle through, past, under or over the opposing team, to touch the ball down on their opponents' mat. Time and again I found my way through the heaving mass of bodies and touched down. I suspect the rest of the class were concentrating on the struggle whereas I had the object of the game always in mind. So too years later here in the work of the education centre I had a limited goal, but I stuck to it like a terrier; if I met opposition, as we all did from time to time, I would come back and back from different angles.

One of the angles of the work was writing. Father Bullen told a visiting publisher about my Widnes workcards, and before long a simplified version of them was published, then another set. My main colleague from the Widnes school's religious education department, Pat Melvin, collaborated in the published workcards: she had also taught English, and had deliberately blurred the frontiers between the two disciplines to the benefit of both. Having once gained the interest of a good publisher, I soon found myself writing a little book on forgiveness. One day it had occurred to me that all the different talks and homilies I was accustomed to give on the subject of forgiveness could be put together to make a small book. I was granted one day off per week from the Centre till it was written.

Besides visiting the four hundred or so schools of the arch-diocese in turn, the team of us priests and Sisters there at the Centre also undertook to help parishes when preparations were in hand for the first celebration of the sacraments of the Eucharist and Reconciliation. We were often invited at these times to give talks to the parents of the children concerned. In many parishes, and more often in inner city parishes than in the country, one or other or both of the parents had been estranged from the Church or afraid to frequent the sacraments for years. Many of them had been estranged in the first place over a mistaken understanding of the Church's teaching. Very many had stopped going to Communion from the day their divorce came through, even though they had never remarried; and many more had let more than a year go by without coming to the Sacrament of Reconciliation, and thought they had thereby committed a mortal sin and so were damned to hell as far as the Church was concerned. On these and many other of their worries we were able to ease their minds, and help them to find their own conscience blessed within the Church's teaching. They were particularly thrilled to hear that we go to the Sacrament of Reconciliation to celebrate the fact that God has already forgiven us. Many were so delighted they came straight after the talk, cup of tea and questions, to celebrate their own forgiveness in the sacrament.

In the early 1970s there were several priests in the community where I lived in St Francis Xavier's parish, so my help was not much needed at home. In the course of the ten years I did celebrate Mass with the home parish, and got to know and love many of the parishioners, but I also made firm friends in many other places in the diocese: the residents and staff of the Leonard Cheshire Home then situated at Springwood Park, the Sisters at Bellerive Convent, the Sisters and Residents at the Centre for Adult Blind and at the same Sisters' school for blind and partially sighted children. I sang dozens of concerts each year with the guitar, at these places and at other residential homes for children. On my Saturday free day I would more often than not go to Blackbrook House School, a community home for girls run by the Daughters of Charity. I reckoned that from the age of eleven until I was thirty-two I had lived in communities exclusively male, so it was high time I spent some days in a community predominately female. God loves all his children: male and female he made them. So I did what I could to help the work of the school by showing in one they knew to be a priest a kindly face of God, never disapproving, always accepting. On those Saturday afternoons the school minibus was often reserved for the use of whichever house-unit I was spending the day with, and we went (always with a Staff member of course) to Delamere Forest or Manchester Airport or Speke Hall or climbing up Rivington Pike, or anywhere that would seem like freedom after the confines of a community home. I am sure the Sisters and Staff realized they were giving me something of greater value than anything I might be giving the girls: a Catholic priest has no children of his own, so he must rely upon others to trust him with their children. I shall always be grateful for the trust placed in me by parents of the families I have visited and the staffs of the schools and children's homes I have made my own on my days off over many years.

Soon after half-way through my time at St Francis Xavier's, Archbishop Derek Worlock succeeded Archbishop Beck on the latter's retirement; the number of priests in our parish was reduced, and we became part of a deanery team responsible for several inner city parishes. This was for me too an opportunity to get to know all the priests, sisters and key lay workers of the deanery, and an ever-increasing circle of friendly faces of the wider neighbourhood. It also meant that I came in for an occasional dose of the bitter opposition the deanery clergy and their supporters experienced for 'betraying' the parishes as they had been for a hundred and forty years. Much of the bitterness had by this time gone out of the opposition we school advisers met in some of the schools. In the early days I for one would occasionally come home to the office shaking like a leaf after facing a bombardment of bitter accusations of heresy, disloyalty and malice in one or other of the schools as if we were deliberately destroying the work of God. We had to keep reminding ourselves not to counter fear by arrogance: there were quite enough arguments in Scripture, Church documents and in the writings of the early Fathers of the Church to leave with the schools as a reminder, without getting cross about the situation. One remembers scars, but of course the vast majority of the schools gave us a warm welcome, and please God that welcome will always be my lasting memory of school visits.

One could say that the work of the Centre which most closely approached the ideal of catechesis was the tuition we and various other colleagues gave for the Catholic Teachers' Religious Certificate. This certificate had to be obtained by any teacher intending to teach religious education in a Catholic school. Catholic Colleges of Education saw to it that their student teachers obtained it in college. Our course of tuition was devised for those teachers who had not been to a Catholic college, or who wanted to bring their familiarity with their religion up to date in line with the Second Vatican Council (1962–65). The numbers in any tutorial group were small and the meetings frequent enough to bring about a certain intimacy and trust, the course was well designed to go the heart of the matter and work outwards from there, and I am sure it was a real reconversion for many of the teachers. Certainly it opened my own eyes to many an important truth because the questions, comments and findings of the teachers forced me to think again.

In 1975 my sister and brother and I had another sorrow when our mother died. After our father's death she continued to live alone until the time came when her memory was going and her friends and neighbours felt they could, quite suddenly, no longer feel responsible for her. Sister Catherine, the Superior or Sister Servant at Christopher Grange, the Centre for Adult Blind where we Jesuits were chaplains, said she would invite our mother over for a fortnight's holiday, to see how she liked the place. She came and loved the place, and it was six months before she suddenly remembered the fortnight was up. So there she stayed, in the beginning able to do a little shopping for other residents or to take a blind person for a little walk, things like that, but gradually doing less and less. Three years after going to Christopher Grange she died there, a happy and a holy death in her sleep as she would have wished, Sister Lucy being with her to the end. She was buried with our father and their infant daughter at Wrightington. For me the sorrow was gentler, because she had been quietly slipping away for three years.

In that same year Father Bullen left the Centre to become a parish priest. All the time we kept on pushing ahead to provide a complete syllabus and scheme of work for teachers of children from five to sixteen, and all the time we were getting back constructive criticism and suggestions from teachers regarding the books and schemes we had already produced. For a year or two I produced a special newsletter for teachers concerned with the raising of the compulsory minimum school-leaving age from fifteen to sixteen. Then I floated another newsletter for teachers of religious education to pupils aged sixteen to eighteen — simply to share around amongst more schools ideas which some had found to work well. In the revised version of the syllabus for Junior children I was most pleased to be able to insert as a key sentence words to the effect that 'God loves the good child, and the naughty child, and the child in between *equally*; being good is our way of saying "Thank you" to God for loving us no matter what we do'. If I have had one crusade in my priestly life, it has been to make sure the least of the little ones know they are not to be left behind.

Lest anyone think these ten years were all work and no play, I did have a good holiday each year, including four splendid sailing holidays with other young Jesuits. We used to hire a yacht on the River Blackwater in Essex and sail up and down the coast and along the east coast rivers, sleeping and eating on board and making maximum use of the tides. The interplay of winds, tides, the trim of the sails and the design of the hull always fascinated me. For three of these four sailing holidays I was a crew member. For the fourth our regular skipper was unable to come, so rather than lose the holiday I organized the week and became the skipper myself, making sure I had a good handy crew. But I much preferred being a crew member.

When the Jesuit Father Provincial visited us on his annual visitation in 1980, he took my breath away by floating the idea of my becoming the next Novice Master. Twenty-two years had passed since my breakdown, and I seemed to have long been once again strong and healthy. My name had been one of those suggested by his advisers. Perhaps I would like to think about it — but not for this year? Now I had secretly always wanted to be Novice Master some day if God wanted it too, but had thought my breakdown had put an end to all that for ever. Suddenly the desire was revived — would I not be able to tell those young men of the love of God in such a way that they would never have to go through the anguish I had gone through? Would they not carry the Good News with tremendous influence to many others? Yet, was I capable of running a house and coaching the novices, by myself or with others, in all the many aspects of the apostolate of today? Would I be able to set up and monitor the 'experiments' or challenges the present Novice Master had set up or developed? Was this to be one of those exceptional cases in which I was born to be a leader? I did not know the answers.

At all events, I heard no more about it from the Provincial, and settled back into what was to be my final year with the Christian Education Centre: mainly spent by me in producing a personal catechism later published as *Abba! Father!*

3·'MY YOKE IS EASY AND MY BURDEN LIGHT'

Turning now to some of the passages of Scripture which seem to express better than I can the driving force behind these years of my apostolate, I would begin by picking out the call of the prophet Jeremiah. Called by Yahweh, he tried to express his own feelings of inadequacy: 'I said, "Ah, Lord Yahweh; look, I do not know how to speak: I am a child!"'

> But Yahweh replied,
> 'Do not say, "I am a child".
> Go now to those to whom I send you
> and say whatever I command you . . .' (Jeremiah 1:6f.).

The mother of Jesus said to the servants at the wedding in Cana, 'Do whatever he tells you' (John 2:5). There was nothing for it but to be unafraid and take whatever I had, five loaves and two fishes or whatever, and begin to share it round among those to whom I was sent.

For a long time now I have been convinced that in God when he speaks to us, 'send' and 'call' are somehow the same reality. The Son of God was indeed *sent* down the mountainside (to use the image of the steps down the side of the Rock that I have been employing) to pick up fallen humanity and bring us with him to the top, but in my own case I seem to have been *called* when I was at the foot of the mountain and later, in Christ, *called* to gather up as many lost travellers as I can find on my journey back to God. I have never been sent back down the mountain, only called towards the Father with the request to bring as many others with me as I can. At least, that is what it feels like. The chapters I go to, thinking of these things, are those containing the Last Supper discourse in St John (John 13 – 17). The prodigal son has a desire to serve as he heads for home, but in the end the only service he is allowed to give is the ever-shining example of trustfully going home with the desire to serve (cf. Luke 15, compare verses 19 and 21f.).

In St Mark's version of the curing of Peter's mother-in-law 'the fever left her and she began to wait on them' (Mark 1:31). In my case something far worse than a fever had left me, and I felt a similar urge to be of service to Jesus and to the community of the faith. There was no rush into action in the early days of my ministry, and I still had plenty of time to ponder the things that had happened to me in my life, matching them all the time with the words of Scripture to find the meaning of what had happened, as seen through the eyes of Jesus. Mary his mother was a quiet reminder of the value of pondering surprising things that happen, and treasuring prophetic words that are occasionally spoken to us (cf. Luke 1:29; 2:19, 50). In the secrecy of my heart I drew great strength from the special moments I have mentioned in my story, when God seemed to come into my house without having to open the door (cf. John 20:26–28), like the greater understanding of the Trinity which came to me in the philosophers' chapel. Within my heart I was always able to answer anybody who challenged me or accused me of this or that by applying to them the words of St Peter: 'You must judge whether in God's eyes it is right to listen to you and not to God. We cannot promise to stop proclaiming what we have seen and heard' (Acts 4:19f.).

As the years of priesthood went by, I became more and more convinced that the phenomenon in the gospels known by the name of the Messianic Secret is there for our imitation, and does not exist solely in the life of Jesus. St Paul tells that in our minds we must be the same as Christ Jesus, who though his state was divine did not cling to his equality with God, but emptied himself to assume the condition of a slave and become as men are (cf. Philippians 2:5ff.). If we must be the same in our minds, then it follows that we, though we are children of God, must empty ourselves, not clinging to our status as children, to become slaves on the pattern of Christ. Jesus in his public ministry would not allow anyone or anything to say openly who he was (Mark 1:24f.) until the right moment came (Mark 14:62). On his way back to the Father, he kept it a secret that he was the Messiah, the divine Son of God, and treated himself as the Servant instead. We too, in imitation of Christ, should 'love to be unknown and to be counted for nothing' (as the author of *The Imitation of Christ* puts it), knowing in our heart of hearts that we are children of God and each loved by God as much as anyone else in the world. We are to hide our own God-given status and use all our energies in showing to those without hope that *they* are children of God. When someone else irritates me or offends me, the solution Jesus offers is that I should say to myself,

73

'This one is God's daughter, that one is God's son. For the sake of winning them over to God's ways, I am God's servant. I shall say nothing: a servant does not answer back to the king's daughter or the king's son!' I may be badly hurt, in which case like Jesus I complain to my Father in heaven (cf. Luke 22.44) — but to the king's daughter or the king's son I try not to complain.

In my ministry to other people I was finding that my own new gift of being free from scruples was making an immeasurable difference. I found I could help poor burdened sufferers to drop their heavy loads. After all, if Jesus' yoke is easy and his burden light, then any yoke that is hard and any burden that is heavy that *can* be dropped *may* be dropped, since it cannot be of Jesus (cf. Matthew 11.28ff.). Once we know how to call God *'Abba!'* and refuse to take any other master but him, we are freed from the intolerable strain of trying to serve two masters (Matthew 6:24). Jesus the Servant of Yahweh is our mirror of freedom (cf. James 1:25; 2:12). Surely it is bringing Good News to the poor (Isaiah 61:1) to tell them their sins are already forgiven as far as God is concerned (Mark 2:5), as they most surely are. Who could possibly say when it was that the father of the prodigal son and the elder brother first began to forgive both of his sons? There never was a time when they were unforgiven, as far as he was concerned.

As servants we do not merit any reward (cf. Luke 17:7–10). We do far better for ourselves if we do not hold out for any reward, but wait instead for our inheritance. Even if we feel we have spent up our inheritance, is not our Father's assured welcome enough for us (Luke 15:31f.)?

4·CONFIDENCE WITH PEACE

The keynote of these adult or 'middle' years in the lives of most people, whether or not they would see themselves as religious, is confidence, confidence with peace. I imagine they would one day look back on those years as the golden years, the years of full maturity. Accordingly the time of life I have dubbed 'Crusade' may be a shorter or much longer period in different people's lives, and may come early in life or later. It may have little obvious connection with religion, or religion may be seen to be at the very

heart of existence. Probably, like myself, others too find themselves with stronger convictions, about politics, about religion,
about family life. They are able now to know their own minds
and follow their own conscience with conviction but a certain
tenderness and tolerance for others who hold different opinions
or who seem weakly to follow the crowd.

For those who are overtly religious in their motivation, there
is less alarm now at the blindness that seemed to veil their eyes
so that they could no longer see Jesus 'out there', but must find
him within themselves, looking out through their own eyes. Jesus
has not gone; quite the contrary, he has come to stay. There is
a saying I once heard from someone living in Liverpool 8, the
district where many black Liverpudlians live: 'Act locally; think
globally'. As we reach maturity in Christ we are fully in touch
with our local situation, but our hearts reach out and see the
world-wide implications of what we are trying to do on a small
local scale. Ideas and reality begin to interlock in our minds and
hearts.

Most people, though they might not recognize the fact, have
a crusade of some sort, and it will have universal application.
Someone cares for the handicapped, someone else campaigns
for the hungry, or for the aged. A business man or woman can
see the wider benefits to the world of their business, a tradesman
or woman can see the blessings of their trade. Professional men
and women have an ideal for their own profession, to do with
making the world a better place for its inhabitants. Those who
are unhappy in their present lives are often so because they have
a better ideal, and cannot see their way to achieving it. All are
stewards of the earth, servants of the Creator. I am not talking
about those who live for purely selfish ambitions, but those who
have accepted their own weakness and who now wish to help
others who are weak. Their reward is in seeing beauty created
and disease, poverty and hatred lessened. Hence they are willing
to take some of the hatred that comes their way, and meet it with
forgiveness.

Adults at this stage of their lives generally rely less and less
on new reading or new information. Look at any family's bookshelves, and see how many of the books date from recent years.
Usually nothing like as many as the books from earlier years.
Among the many reasons why parents (and the same applies
to many priests' bookshelves!) have not bought so many books

lately is the good reason that they have come to possess clear and gentle but powerful convictions which no longer need much adjustment. One who knows what love is no longer needs many books about it. One who has learnt to pray will only be confused by many books about prayer.

I hope that among the strong convictions of parents will always be the conviction that their own hearts are to be trusted, and that they can safely teach their children: 'God loves the naughty child, and the good child, and the child in between *equally*. We try to be good, as a way of saying "thank you" to God.'

VI

The Long Siege

1·INTO THE CAVE

The next surprise on the way up the Mediterranean Steps was the discovery that what I had taken for the summit was in fact a good deal short of the summit — a surprise well known to climbers of hills and mountains. Instead I was faced with another cliff rising on my left: rather as I had been with the cliff I had encountered below where the steps were leading downwards; this one, a hundred feet high, leaned over the path in a most uncomfortable fashion, but at least this time the steps were going upwards. There was every reason to expect that once past the cliff I would see the way zig-zagging clear to the top.

But there was another anxiety ahead, of which the cave I had recently passed reminded me. I remembered that on a previous visit to Gibraltar I had walked to the ridge at the summit by way of the metalled road running up the less sheer western slopes to the military installations and other buildings at the top. I had leaned over a wall to gaze at the view on the eastern side. A good way down four people were climbing up what must have been the Mediterranean Steps, coming towards me. They were two young men and two young women: I guessed they were two servicemen and their wives. Still a good way below me they produced a torch from a knapsack and disappeared into the rock-face. After what seemed a long time they reappeared behind and below me on the western side. I went down to look at the place they had come out of, and soon discovered it was by no means a straight tunnel through from one side to another: it was more like a maze at a fairground. I was nearly lost in it there and then. Well now, my problem as I myself climbed up the Steps was that I had no torch. The last cave had been a dead-end, only a few feet deep. Perhaps the next cave, the one the four young people had gone through, was the only way to the top from where I stood?

I did not fancy going all the way back down those steps: with my poor sense of balance I would have had to go down most of them backwards! But it was still hours away from darkness, and I would *rather go backwards down a thousand steps than lose my way in the middle of the Rock somewhere in total darkness. However, having come this far I could only go ahead and find out whether the way the others had gone was the only way, or whether the steps carried on in daylight past and above the cave as I hoped.*

With my eyes down for fear of the cliff above me (strange how the world closes in around us when we are anxious) I carried on climbing, just looking ahead from time to time. Sure enough, there was what must be the cave, and the path led right into it.

2·SABBATICAL TRAVELS, NOVICE MASTER, AND TENSIONS TOO MUCH FOR ME

When Father Provincial came back to visit us in the spring of 1981 he asked me again, now formally, if I would like my name to go forward, to take over from the present Novice Master in September of the following year, provided Archbishop Worlock would release me from my work in the diocese. I said I would: I now felt I was strong enough to cope with running a house, and in addition to the reasons I had immediately thought of for saying yes a year ago, I was also delighted at being asked to take on something so central to the work of the British Province. These past twelve years had been exciting to live through, and the teamwork at the education centre had been with as good a set of companions as anyone could desire, but it was all at one remove from what most British Jesuits were working on. I always felt slightly a stranger in St Francis Xavier's parish because I was not working with the deanery team much, and slightly a stranger at the Centre because I was the only Jesuit there.

As to the running of the novitiate house: ten years earlier I had turned down a request to take on a University Chaplaincy mainly because there was a large 'plant' attached to the job, and at that stage I did not feel like spending half my time as a kind of hotel manager while still unsure in my mind of the priorities within Christianity itself. Now I was more sure of my goals.

When my proposed leaving of Liverpool and the change of superiors at Harborne in Birmingham (where the novitiate now was) had been approved by Archbishop Worlock and the Jesuit Father General respectively, and was made public, I had a few months in which to say my goodbyes to Liverpool and all my colleagues and friends there. The Archbishop said kind things to me about how grateful he was for what I had been able to do in the diocese, and he wrote a letter to the same effect which I keep as a souvenir. *Abba! Father!* appeared in print. I had a holiday, and my last task for the Christian Education Centre was the very pleasant one of visiting Gibraltar to help with a course for teachers. The primary schools in Gibraltar, where teaching is through English, had been using our Liverpool syllabus and schemes of work for several years, and every now and then they liked to have colleagues from Liverpool over to exchange ideas. This was the second time I had been one of those chosen to go. (On one of these visits we visitors were shown the path to the Mediterranean Steps.)

My plan for the sabbatical year I was granted in preparation for taking on the novitiate was, first of all, to spend from October to Christmas at St Beuno's reading up again and more deeply about St Ignatius, the foundation of the Society of Jesus, its constitutions and its history. Next, in January, I planned to visit the Birmingham novitiate briefly to say Hello, and then the Irish novitiate; and in March I had been invited to direct four novices of the Faithful Companions of Jesus through their thirty-day retreat at Broadstairs in Kent. Soon after that I was to visit the United States to see some Jesuit novitiates there; and finally to move in to Birmingham and understudy with the present Novice Master. If I were planning the year again with hindsight, I would have moved to Birmingham as soon as I could, in October at the latest, understudied right away but with time for reading, paid particular attention to the novices' experiments (what, where, with which people as hosts and supervisors), directed the Broadstairs long retreat, and postponed the visits abroad till I knew what I was doing at home. However, that is, as they say, water under the bridge. With God, no 'might have beens'.

I enjoyed the visit to the United States as much as anything else in that exciting year of preparation. The novitiates I visited were in Philadelphia, Denver, Portland and Santa Barbara, so I saw in a short time a varied selection of scenery, from the spectacular to the suburban and inner city. Springtime in the Rockies near Denver was spectacular, but with carpets of little flowers like crocuses at the other end of the scale. My favourite spot of all was a log cabin I was taken to on the Oregon coast, surrounded by miles of trees and with its own panorama window looking out on a river mouth, sand dunes and the Pacific Ocean beyond, where the only other people we saw all the day were a man and wife going out fishing in a small boat in the morning and coming back at tea-time. The novices wherever I went were superb cooks, and their cooking reflected their many different national origins. On the more pertinent business of what makes a good novice master and a good novice, I was given most generous time and help and encouragement by the four Novice Masters, their fellow team-members and by the novices themselves. Jesuits from the States are most generous wherever in the world one meets them, but on their home territory the great generosity takes one's breath away.

While in the States I was delighted to meet up again with a family who had befriended me in Brussels, now with two boys as well as the two girls they already had in Brussels. They were living in Annapolis, Maryland, only a few hours' bus ride from Philadelphia, so I went and spent a happy week with them and had a taste of American family life and parish life. As I write the parents and the boys are in El Salvador, the parents working with Catholic Relief Services among that country's all too many refugees.

Then it was back to England and Birmingham, to learn as much as I could in a short time from the present Novice Master. On 8 September 1982 he handed over to me. For two months all seemed to go well. As far as I was concerned, all was going splendidly, and I felt more completely alive and fulfilled than at any time in my life before. The days were full — too full — and I was not sleeping well; another worry was the arrangements for the novices' experiments after Christmas, which I had no time to get organized because of the imminent Long Retreat for the first year novices. But apart from these I felt splendid, like a charioteer doing well.

The crash came during the Long Retreat. In November I was with the first year novices, and two others from the Birmingham community, in the Jesuit house in Barmouth, a lovely house overlooking Cardigan Bay. The first week of the novices' retreat complete, we had a free day, and on the morning of the first day of the second week — suddenly in a moment the whole elation that had filled me more and more in the past four months and longer turned to total revulsion. There was no time to explain, to ask for help, to make alternative arrangements, I just had to get out of that house and that situation and the vice-like grip of that future as a Novice Master. I went out of the house as if blown from it – no coat if I remember rightly, no gloves, no luggage, no money. I walked down the road to the town centre, turned to follow the road up the river estuary, and began to feel a little better. A few miles along the road I called in at a house where I had once stayed a few days, and the warden kindly let me use his telephone without commenting on my obviously distressed state — he just showed me to the phone and gave me a cup of tea.

I called the novitiate house in Birmingham, and told my assistant who was there at the time that I could not carry on, something in me had snapped. He reacted very quickly, told me not to worry, he would see to it that the Long Retreat, the experiments and everything else were taken care of. Would I be able to get myself back to the Barmouth house, and wait for him there? I said I thought I could, and we rang off. However, I had not reckoned with the force of the revulsion that was in me. I managed to walk back to Barmouth, but as soon as I turned the bend in the road that brought me face to face with the hill up to the Jesuit house, I could go no further. It felt like an invisible wall. Determined to get back up there if it killed me, I tried again, and managed to get as far as the barber's shop in the town. I went in, flopped in one of his swivel-chairs (luckily the shop was empty except for the startled barber himself), and asked him to telephone for help. He did that, and eventually two policemen drove me back to the brethren. As the two policemen escorted me one on either side to the door of our house, I remember remarking to the two of the community who came out to meet us 'Funny! Crucified between two policemen.' All the way up the hill you would have said there was only one policeman, the driver: the other was *hiding* behind my car-seat. I suppose that is standard procedure in such cases.

That night was a difficult one to get through. My assistant had arrived with a young Jesuit Brother from Birmingham, and he arranged to sleep in the same room in case I should need help or be unable to cope with the length of the night. I keep searching around for metaphors to describe feelings: this night it was as if I were being spun up and down the axis of the earth, reaching the surface with unspeakable effort and then being dragged down the axis again by gravity. I suppose I was striving to regain stability.

The next day the two who had come from Birmingham drove me up to St Beuno's where I had spent my tertianship year, and soon the local doctor there asked me if I would go into the North Wales Hospital where they would help me regain stability. I agreed. The first week at the hospital was spent in the secure unit, called Bryn Golau, 'The Hill of Light'. Apart from the emotional turmoil inside of me, I enjoyed that week and have happy memories of it. The staff were wonderful, at all levels. I had many visitors in that week — some dearly loved and interwoven in my life for years and years, like my brother, of course, and my brother-in-law (who encouraged me greatly by being impressed with the place and the staff), and the Jesuit who had been chaplain at Glasgow when I lived at the chaplaincy — some whom I had never met before. This breakdown for some reason sharpened my eyesight and sense of colour in ways that were breathtakingly beautiful to behold, and the house on the Hill of Light had been very sensitively planned so that the colour schemes matched the activities that went on in each room — bright colours in the dining room, restful colours in the lounge, black and white predominant in the sleeping quarters — that sort of thing. I shall never forget the colours of the North Wales countryside one sunny, frosty morning when a few of us were escorted on a short walk: I have never seen Wales look more beautiful than on that day.

The patients in Bryn Golau reacted dramatically to their treatment at times: a poor soul would come in one day and walk around like a robot, with leaden eyes — and a couple of days later would look perfectly normal and happy. I suppose my own cure was rapid too, because after a week I was transferred to an open ward in the main building of the hospital. Life there was not as stimulating as it had been in the secure unit, but we all made progress, and after another three weeks I was discharged, back to St Beuno's. On the final day the charge nurse told me my pills were changed: from now on I would have pills containing lithium carbonate, and I would have to come back every month to another hospital for a blood test, to make sure the level of lithium was not so high as to be dangerous nor so low as to be useless. My heart sank: by now all the elation of being Novice Master had evaporated. From being over-excited I was now slightly depressed and daily growing more depressed. The thought of having pills that involved a monthly blood test *and* a six-monthly visit to the psychiatrist, and which therefore must be expected to weigh me down for years to come, did nothing to cheer me up.

These were the forms the depression took when I was back in St Beuno's. I no longer trusted myself to drive a car — that took about three months to overcome. I could hardly face the strangers, of whom there were naturally many coming and going in a retreat house and conference centre. I could scarcely hold a pen to make it write legibly. I dreaded letters and other Christmas mail coming, because I did not feel up to answering any but the most essential. This meant I felt I was losing touch: friend of all the world, crusader for the little ones, could no longer cope with all the world or even the little ones. I could not pass a day or even half a day without pleading for sympathetic company, and I will ever remember the kindness with which various friends popped in from time to time, and indeed popped out again if they found the time was not ripe. I could not say Mass, nor could I even sit still for the length of a Mass celebrated by somebody else. The longer Sunday Mass was agony. The thought of ever preaching or giving talks seemed quite out of the question; even a homily was way beyond my powers. All Scripture references and theological ideas were either gone from my memory or scattered beyond recall. I could not read a book for weeks, even the lightest of novels. I could not stay up long enough for the 9 o'clock news or any evening recreation with the community. I had to force myself to wash, shave, bathe, wash my hair. Heaven knows how many cigarettes I smoked, because I could not sit still even in my room otherwise than when smoking or talking with someone. What prayers I could say were one line long, usually from the more anguished of the psalms.

I was very touched that Father Provincial came in person to tell me someone else had been appointed Novice Master: the Long Retreat had been completed by the last Novice Master but one, my predecessor was completing the rest of the year with the novices, and then the new man would take over. I should have been relieved, as I now am in retrospect, but the news hurt at the time. So I was grateful the Provincial came himself to tell me.

I should add, too, that with all this depression in my heart, the pain was nothing like as deadly as the fear of hell from which I was freed twenty-odd years earlier. The servant now was blind, deaf, dumb, paralysed, but never damned, only useless. Then, I had to hide my uselessness, out of fear; now, I moaned about it to anyone that would listen! There was only one cure for the present depression, to wait as patiently as I could, to trust my closest advisers, to trust the doctors. A daily visitor, a former shipmate of sailing days who was a counsellor on the staff at St Beuno's, was a marvellous tonic, very patient too when the cure was slow in coming. He helped me to see I was not blind, or deaf, or paralysed, but simply fogbound. One day the fog would lift and I would see, hear and walk once more. Or else I was like a person suddenly plunged into a dark room, who for a time can see nothing; but then the little light there is turns out to be enough to get around with. Perhaps the thing he said which cheered me more than anything was his quiet insistence that I was not a 'failed Novice Master' but a perfectly good one, much appreciated by the novices.

As the weeks turned into months I began to perk up a little. I had a very good book on British wild flowers, and began to take longer walks identifying the flowers that appeared in the hedgerows as spring approached. I was asked to prepare a young boy and a young girl who came to Mass on Sundays, for their First Communion, and that all passed off very happily. One of the Sisters, who had often driven me to and from the doctor's and helped me to endure the waiting there, got me driving a car again. I started writing a book, eventually published as *The Cup that I Drink*. My first attempt was to rewrite the book on St Mark which had never seen the light of day, but that came to nothing after only a few pages. Yet only a month after leaving hospital I began on the book about the chalice, and it practically wrote itself: I had had it in mind for many years. I would scrawl a page in handwriting that only I could read and then slowly type it up. By summer time I was beginning to help with one or two directed retreats.

Father Provincial again made a generous gesture by coming from London to meet me half way, at Crewe no less. We talked over whether I should stay at St Beuno's or move somewhere else, and we came down in favour of Loyola Hall. The Superior and Retreat Director there agreed, and in September 1983 I moved myself and all my worldly goods to Loyola — much changed in some respects from when I left there in 1969, but still with a feeling of home about it for me. I was welcomed with open arms by the Jesuits and Loreto Sisters (of the Institute of the Blessed Virgin Mary) who lived and worked there.

I was still convalescent, and should have distrusted my own strong desire to come off the lithium pills. Through a sad misunderstanding, I was able to wean myself off them, as I thought of it, and, such is the nature of the illness in its early days, I did not recognize the growing symptoms as symptoms of another breakdown. I must have felt the illness coming back, though, because I had a sense of racing to finish the book on the chalice before it was too late. I did finish it, but very soon afterwards I became unnaturally euphoric, for me. The community looked after me for a while — this time it was the meals brought to my room which tasted like heaven, especially the breakfasts, though they were no more exotic than cornflakes, toast and a boiled egg. After nights of sleeplessness and mental turmoil they tasted wonderful, served up as they were with a friendly conversation and a warm smile. While there in my room I sifted through all my belongings, throwing out some notes, keeping others, throwing away old photographs if they were of people I could no longer carry: God would look after them now. I know I spoke a lot about 'if I should die today', but I was not being morbid, only using the thought of death as a yardstick of what to keep and what to let go of. I wanted to travel light from now on, emotionally light. While all this was going on I know I must have been a trial to the brethren, especially the three who looked after me. I was resisting the medicines they had to give me, because I had an ill-founded conviction the medicines were changing my personality in some subtle way. Eventually I gave my reluctant consent to going into a local hospital, because by this time I could no longer cope with my turbulent feelings. This was the middle of February 1984.

The first week in this hospital was as unbearable as the first week in previous mental hospitals: music that played on the radio speakers of a morning and afternoon was helpful to me, though it made me feel like dancing to it all the time; but the nights were unbearably long and I kept trying to get up and being sent back to bed like a naughty boy. Anything on television in the evenings was either unbearably personal, or unbearably beautiful, or unbearably horrific; games of cards or dominoes went on unbearably long; waiting for visitors was unbearable. Fellow patients had problems of their own, so one day they could be friendly, the next distant and withdrawn. The food was good, well cooked and plenty of it; only the waiting for the next meal was unbearable!

What was going on inside me in my own feelings was like this:
I was no longer being spun up and down the earth's axis (or had
the earth been spinning around me?), but I was on or near the
surface, looking for my own place on it. Once it was found, I felt
right: from here, my own place, I could for the first time ever be in
the right relationship with everyone else. Friends and dear ones
at a distance were no longer at a distance, or rather distance was
not significant any more. I remember I made up a poem about a
waterfall, in which I was a droplet of water, and whether I was
falling headlong, or I was stationary and the rocks were rushing
upwards did not seem to matter much any more.

As in previous times spent in hospital — I was beginning to
recognize the pattern — after the first week of unbearable excitement came the beginnings of depression. By now the psychiatrist
had put me back on the lithium treatment, the effect of which
is to stabilize the emotions at a healthy mean between manic
over-excitement and deep depression. I was coming to appreci-
ate this lithium, and to see it not as a strangler of emotion but
as a liberator, like the rails on a high footbridge. But the lithium
takes weeks or months to build up to its full power, and in the
meantime I was unbearably depressed by the time I came home
to Loyola after three or four weeks of hospital. No need to go
through again all the things I could not do, like driving a car and
all the rest. The main burden of sharing my burden fell on the
ever kind and willing Superior, a class-mate of mine from school
days. I would keep reaching a point when I felt like screaming,
then I would go in search of him, to listen and to reassure me.
He kept gently saying back to me what he knew was dearest to
my heart, that God is my 'Abba' as he is Jesus', that there is no
measuring of merits, that it didn't really matter terribly if I never
managed another stroke of work for the rest of my life, but that
he himself was quite sure my talents would revive when they
had had a rest. When I now think back on those days, it seems
to me that I was again a city under siege: the water, the spring
of fresh water, was still there but I could neither see it nor reach
it nor hear it, let alone taste it. My companion when I called on
him would go to my own spring, fill a cup with cold water, and
give it to me to drink. As another St Ignatius, Bishop of Antioch,
wrote to the Christians in Rome on his way to martyrdom there
at the beginning of the second century AD: 'In me there is left
no spark of desire for earthly things, but only a murmur of

living water that whispers within me, "Come to the Father"'. The Sisters of Notre Dame at Standish took up the good work for a few weeks, giving me the same living water from my own well. The attitude of all the rest of the community at Loyola Hall was in line with the Superior's lead: never a word of complaint at having to carry me, never any pressure to get back to work, always cheerful acceptance as if nothing in me was changed. The same goes for Jesuit and other visitors who treated me the same as ever, which to me was a gift more precious than gold just then.

Healing came in time, and my spirits were further raised by my being transferred to the care of a Catholic psychiatrist at the Royal Liverpool Hospital who had heard of my plight earlier and kindly offered help. We got along very well, and I began to think my troubles were finally over. I had not reckoned with the book *The Cup That I Drink*. While I was in hospital the last time the manuscript had been taken to the Provincial for him to have it censored. Books written by Jesuits must go through a Jesuit screening as well as that of the bishop of the territory on which the publishing house lies, so it is usually better to get the Jesuit screening over first and then offer the script to a publisher with no strings attached to it. The Loyola Hall Superior waited several months before giving me the script back; not that the comments were hostile, but there was a fair number of them and I was obviously not fit to cope with complications until near the end of that year of 1984.

Then on 27 December came the sudden and shattering news that my brother-in-law had died in the night. He was a consultant physician greatly loved and respected, at 69 years old not long retired. Family and friends came to rally round my sister in what inadequate ways we could, and being still in my convalescence I was free to stay on for a few weeks to be company, someone to help with the shopping and be the first to answer the phone and doorbell.

Back at Loyola in February I set about revising the script of the chalice book, and found that quite unexpectedly it raised severe tensions in me. The censors (three of them, no less, which didn't make things simpler) did not insist on corrections, but obviously they knew what they were talking about and I would be silly not to pay good attention. But there were one or two comments that kept reappearing in different forms, which seemed to me at the time, in my emotional state, to cut at the very heart of the book, and not just the book — the comments seemed to cut at the heart of my crusade for the little ones, and therefore at the heart of me. To answer them properly and defend my own position would take another book demanding expertise in Scripture I did not possess. I was defending an instinctive interpretation I just *knew* was right. Somehow in quick time lest I fail to complete the revision before sickness overtook me again, I reached a version that skirted round the objections without giving up what I knew was true, packed it up and sent it off to the publishers.

But the tensions had been too much for me. A few days later I was in hospital again.

3·'MY ONE COMPANION IS DARKNESS . . . LET ME KNOW YOUR LOVE'

The time usually comes when within our own lives Jesus the good shepherd is sent back down the hill to gather up the lost sheep. He may even have to die, in us, in resisting the wolf that would destroy the sheep and lambs the Father has given him (cf. John 10:11ff.). The wolf is the spirit that would measure merits and put conditions on God's love for even the least desirable of the little ones. We would like to go straight ahead in our strength and climb straight into heaven, knowing as we do that we shall be welcome — but the Father asks us to accept the cross of Jesus. To us it will seem that the sheep are being scattered because the shepherd is stricken (cf. Mark 14:27, where Jesus quotes Zechariah 13:7), stricken by God, what is more; but Jesus reassures us that afterwards, and because of the cross, the flock will be gathered in him and led into heaven (cf. Mark 14:28). This is a hard lesson, a lesson which of its very nature is too difficult to understand at the time when we are suffering.

Jesus reassures us in the words with which he prepares us to expect trouble: 'The disciple is not superior to his teacher, nor the slave to his master. It is enough for the disciple that he should grow to be like his teacher, and the slave like his master' (Matthew 10:24f.). 'Was it not ordained that the Christ should suffer and so enter into his glory?' The servant, like the master, must expect to be a 'stone rejected by the builders' and to be like 'gold . . . tested by fire' (cf. 1 Peter 2:8; 1:7).

I am talking now of a distress which overtakes us *after* we had thought all was at long last going well with our lives. So it was that I found appropriate the prayer of the blind Bartimaeus, 'Master, let me see again' (Mark 10:51); 'Master, you opened my eyes once and, as I thought, for ever. But now I am blind again.' Or the father of the epileptic boy: 'I believe; help my unbelief', or 'I do have faith. Help the little faith I have' (Mark 9:24). What I thought was enough, is not enough (I have gold, but it is unrefined).

The death and resurrection of Jesus was compared even by himself to the destruction of Jerusalem in 587 BC, the Exile of God's people to Babylon, followed by their return from Exile, and the rebuilding of the city walls and Temple (cf. John 2:19). This seeming death-blow to God's Chosen People involved a different kind of slavery from the original slavery in Egypt from which they had escaped in the Exodus. In Egypt for four hundred years they had been 'no people', till God called them out to be his people; in 587 BC they were a proud people with a line of kings arching over five hundred years. The slavery of the people in Egypt had been harsh, and God's deliverance spectacular; in 587 the death was inflicted on the people themselves, not on their enemies. Across the Red Sea they were called by a God they hardly knew; in 587 the God who had loved them since the creation of the world suddenly let them die and did nothing. Jeremiah the prophet saw what was coming in 587; when the people saw it too and began to panic, Jeremiah ostentatiously went out and bought a field when everyone else was selling theirs, as a sign that God would never desert them for long and one day they would be back in their own fields again (cf. Jeremiah 32:8). The prophet Ezekiel consoled the people in exile, saying that though their lives and fortunes be as unpromising as a valley full of dry (long-dead) bones, Yahweh would reconstruct the living being and breathe life into it again. He had done it once: why not again? (cf. Ezekiel 37).

The Songs of the Servant of Yahweh embedded in the Book of Isaiah are beautiful and inspiring to read and meditate upon before and after a time of darkness, but they offer surprisingly little comfort in the darkness itself. The first Song (Isaiah 42:1–9) tells how the Servant is loved and chosen by Yahweh and endowed with a spirit of gentleness, but he will persevere till the ends of the earth have heard his message. The second Song (Isaiah 49:1–6)

89

says Yahweh called the Servant before ever he was born. He will lie hidden like a sword in its scabbard or like an arrow in the quiver until the moment when Yahweh's hand draws him forth (as a warrior draws his weapon in the hour of need). The Servant begins to feel weariness, and is consoled by Yahweh.

In the third Song (Isaiah 50:4–9), the Servant is taught how to listen to the wearied and have the right word to speak in reply. He is suffering persecution and is even spat upon. In the fourth Song (Isaiah 52:13 – 53:12) come the verses that remind us so strongly of the crucifixion of Jesus: we read this passage as the first reading on Good Friday at the Liturgy of the Word.

In my prayers at this time I could cope with very little: praying with Jesus, 'Abba! (Father) . . . Please take this cup away from me' (cf. Mark 14:36); praying with the distressed father, 'I believe; help my unbelief' or with Bartimaeus, 'Jesus, let me see again'; praying with Jesus on the cross, 'Father, forgive them' (cf. Luke 23:34) and 'My God, my God, why have you deserted me?' (Mark 15:34) or 'I am thirsty' (John 19:28).

The only part of the daily Prayer of the Church which was anything but a blur on the page to me was the psalm on Tuesday nights ('. . . In the morning let me know your love' — Psalm 143:8) and the psalm on Friday nights, with its last line, 'My one companion is darkness' (Psalm 88:18).

4·LEARNING TO RELY ON GOD ALONE

No one need fear, if they see in their own past lives no remarkable time of suffering, that therefore sorrow is lying in wait for them. They may have had already the worst days they will ever have to endure, and they may like Jesus after the resurrection have made light of what they went through. God never tries anyone beyond their strength: one day we will all live to tell the tale of our lives. So, as I have said, some people may have their worst sufferings early in their lives, and many others have sufferings which are never spectacular but always persistent.

The main characteristic of the kind of suffering the Servant of Yahweh goes through in the prophecies is that the suffering is pointless. For instance, before, a breakdown in health led to a break*through*; this time, there appears to be no future. A business built up over a lifetime crashes; the marriage partner of a lifetime dies almost as soon as he retires; parents discover a son or daughter has committed suicide; ten years short of retirement a breadwinner with a family faces dismissal from work, or sudden redundancy at a time when jobs are scarce; a child has leukaemia; a child is born handicapped. 'I thought I believed; O God, help my unbelief!'

Often in these circumstances there comes a kind of persecution. What I mean is, there is a stigma attached to many of these unmerited sufferings, which is felt by the sufferer simply because he or she is in distress and cannot see straight. In my own case, four out of five of the hospitals I was in were given over exclusively to psychiatric patients, so that the name of the hospital is a standing joke in the neighbourhood. My own laughter is a little brittle when people in all innocence make jokes in my presence about the local psychiatric hospital. They do not mean to hurt me, they just do hurt me for a moment — it feels like a twinge of pain in an old wound. The real place where this stigma did hurt was in the hospital itself, as I said to myself, 'And have I come to this?'.

So also with a loved one who dies before time: could I not have prevented it? Will we never say to one another the things left unsaid because we thought there was no hurry? With a handicapped child: what did we do, to deserve this? Is it in any way our fault? Surely there can be no breakthrough, when a son or daughter has committed suicide, when a child is mentally retarded for life, when a lifetime's work lies in ruins? Perhaps we are driven to shout at God in our hearts, and perhaps that makes us feel guilty. At least it shows we believe in God: nobody rails against a person he does not believe exists. 'I believe . . . I know I do, because I hate you; help my unbelief, to believe again that you love me.' When a person is in distress, he often says the exact opposite of what he really means. 'I hate you' so often means, 'I love you: why did you do this thing to me?'. There is a love/hate relationship with God which can go on for years and which feels unbearable.

Here and there in our anguish we may feel an unexpected nearness to God, a nearness felt not only in our hearts but in coincidences that happen, friends that call to see us just when we were desperate, a word said on the radio that stops us short because it exactly answers what we were just saying to God. Scripture would encourage us to believe that these trials are the kind that take our loved ones away for a time so that we will learn to rely on God alone, dark and invisible though he is. Then God will give us all our loved ones back again, without having done us or them any harm. In the long run, Jesus came to no harm, did he? Nor shall we or those we love.

But this kind of conviction in the power of the resurrection takes its own time, just as things in nature take their own time to come to fruition, just as the refining of gold is not achieved in the twinkling of an eye. We have to keep reminding ourselves that suffering is not a punishment, for past sins or for anything else, any more than prosperity is a reward.

Jesus was taunted on the cross, 'He saved others; he cannot save himself'. In these times of darkness, we seem to hear our friends and foes alike shake their heads and marvel: 'She saved others; why can she not save herself?' or 'He saved others; he has no right to let me down like this'. Our friends are not in fact saying any such thing, but how we need their constant reassurance!

'Walk humbly with your God'

1·OVER THE SUMMIT

I came close up in front of the cave, and saw to my considerable relief that as with the cave lower down there was a path leading into the cave but also another doubling round a hairpin bend and then upwards in broad daylight: the Steps did carry on to the top. I had a look inside the cave, and it was certainly the one the four service people had known their way through to reach the other side: it was like a maze from this end too.

I came again into the fresh air and looked around me. The view upwards was completely open now, short sharp zig-zags of the Steps leading less than a hundred feet upwards to the parapet at the summit. I even recognized the wall at the top as the place where I had leaned over from the other side. The cliff was a thing of the past; I had come round the corner of it and there were no more obstacles. With a light heart I began climbing the remaining steps; I was hot and sticky with perspiration, but that didn't seem to matter any more; it simply provided an excuse for stopping to admire the view and to savour the satisfaction of being 'nearly there'.

The last few turns of the path climb with the Rock on one side and a safe stone wall on the other, so sheer is the fall below. I had the sensation of climbing from the road to the front door of a cottage on a Welsh hillside by a stone-walled garden path.

Then at last here was the summit, and the luxury of having no further to climb. I spent a good time resting and admiring the view, which on that day meant admiring the Rock as seen from the top: breathtaking cliffs one side, lush vegetation sloping down to the city on the other side. Further along the ridge I could see and hear holidaymakers who had come up by the chairlift. I know I neither envied them nor pitied them: I had enjoyed my climb, and they seemed to have enjoyed their ride as they made their way down the hill a little way to have a look inside the spectacular St Michael's Cave. Apart *from the Rock nothing else was visible because of the mist. Africa is often invisible from Gibraltar, but today because of the Levanter even Spain was shrouded in mist.*

After a quarter of an hour or so I set off walking along the metalled road on the western slopes, which winds down this way and then that till it brings the traveller to the city. By this time my friend and host would be beginning to get the dinner ready, to the sound of music most likely.

2·COPING WITH THE 'SICK ROLE' AND WALKING AGAIN

The Royal Liverpool Hospital is a tall new building, and the dining-room window in my ward looked out across the city with the Cathedral of Christ the King prominent in the foreground. The hospital nurses and staff and the chaplains who came in from the cathedral were exceptionally kind to me, in the five days I was there before being discharged back to Loyola Hall. That was in March 1985. The psychiatrist had told me, and now he told me again, that the lithium I was taking regularly could not guarantee I would never have this kind of illness again; it would, however, almost certainly make any future illness less ferocious than the previous ones had been. Sure enough, five days in hospital was better than a month, such as I had had previously.

Another thing the doctor told me, and still tells me, is that I will always be the last to realize I am getting ill. My community can see I am getting over-excited, while I experience only a great sense of well-being.

Why do I make a comparison between this part of my life and the moment of reaching the top of my walk up the Mediterranean Steps, then looking around and starting off downhill towards home? There are many, many reasons. Rightly or wrongly, I feel that life cannot have all that many more distressing surprises to spring on me, and these when they come may be like occasional rises in the road which one encounters on the way downhill, rather than another peak to scale higher than any other I have met so far. I sincerely hope there will be no more visits to hospital as a patient; but even if there are, I have been in wards for mental illness and wards for surgery, and I have been through, again and again, the depression that comes after mental illness. These depressions are shattering enough at first, but the patient eventually comes to *recognize* the first signs of recovery as they occur.

Above all, my ambitions are now much smaller and life-size: having reached too high and found my own limitations, I now aim to 'walk humbly with my God', simply coping with the day-to-day challenges that God puts in my path. To my mind, if we are going to compare the journey to God with climbing a mountain, a comparison so many saints have made, then I would rather think of my path through life as a journey up to the top followed by a journey down the other side and back home. Who, after all, wants to spend an eternity at the top of a mountain, where as often as not there is half a gale blowing and one is enveloped in cloud? Much preferable, surely, to reach the top and then come down again by a different route to a warm house where a warm welcome and a hot meal await us. I was very much aware of God as the Rock under me in the most distressing times of my life, and especially during the five days in the Liverpool hospital, that March of 1985; but what with the strength of the wind and my blindness in the fog and mist (so to speak), I have no desire ever to be back up there — much less any higher. According to my own image, we each have our own mountain to climb, which is another way of saying we each have our own place in the Father's heart, and we each have our own place at the Father's table. I am not called to climb your mountain, nor you mine. There is no race between us, to see who can climb the highest.

At the summit of the Steps I found other holidaymakers, as I have said; only they came up by cable-car. There have been times, when everything was going wrong for me, that it seemed almost everyone else was getting a ride to the top of their own particular mountain — why should I be the one for whom everything went wrong? But in times of better health I decide differently: in the course of a lifetime it probably happens that everyone has to encounter much the same amount of disappointment and distress. One of the features of sorrow is that it attacks us from the very direction we can least cope with. At all events, it is clearly wiser not to judge one another or decide that someone else is getting off too lightly. Who are we, to call God unfair?

A climber who reaches the top of a hill and starts walking down the other side finds he is using different muscles. So in my own life I find it a different kind of strain, but still a strain, to accept what the doctor describes as 'the sick role'. In the year of depression following illness, those who are closest to me, my own family and my religious community, accept readily enough in the kindness of their hearts that I am still ill. For myself, I fancy I would find it easier to accept and live with a broken leg or something visible like that. From now on life needs to be paced differently, as many people suffering from many different illnesses find. As long as a depression lasts, I might as well accept that it is there, as pretend it should be somewhere else and blame myself. As long as I am vulnerable to these recurrent illnesses, I had better avoid the kinds of stress which seem to bring the illnesss on.

Depression after mental illness is not something that can be wished away, as I have discovered. It takes its own time to lift from my heart, regardless of the efforts I may be able to make towards dispelling it. After coming out of the Liverpool Royal early in 1985 I recovered some skills fairly quickly. After two months I was able to give a 'preached retreat', namely a retreat with formal talks, which I had prepared before getting ill. After three months I felt well enough to make a summer holiday worth while. This was the time I accepted a kind invitation from the headmaster of a school in Gibraltar, to come out for a holiday; and this was the time, early June 1985, when I satisfied my curiosity and climbed up the Mediterranean Steps. The idea for this book came to me very soon afterwards. This was the time, too, that I began, in late spring and early summer, to take photographs of wild and cultivated flowers growing in the grounds of Loyola Hall, as well as wild flowers from the walks in our locality. The results gave me great joy and consolation, and stirred me to get out into the fresh air rather than stay indoors all the time.

One by one, old skills come back. Tasks I thought I would never again be able to take on suddenly seem possible again. Skills go underground in illness, and then in their own time they surface once more. Confidence does not come back strongly in every case: some things, like driving a car, I find I can do again in a month or two and the confidence stays with me; other things, like giving talks to people, I may be able to face fairly quickly, but then every subsequent talk for several months to follow needs as much of an act of faith as the first.

This was about as far as I reached in 1985. Early in the New Year of 1986 my improvement suddenly went across the borderline into sickness again, and, as had been predicted by the doctor, I felt fine but it was the community who noticed my old symptoms reappearing. However, this time I was observed in good time, and so I did not have to go back into hospital: I was treated as an out-patient.

To my disappointment, the depression which followed when I came back down to earth again was as stubborn as all the previous depressions had been. This time, as my recovery has gone forward I have been noting the order in which the confidence to do various things has returned. For the first three weeks or so all was gloom and confusion. Then the first blessing to return was the great blessing of sleep. From having totally sleepless nights during the illness, quite quickly came the desire and the ability to sleep half the hours God gives us.

Next came the power to sit still during Mass, such a relief after the desperate restlessness of the sickness. Then I began to be able to celebrate Mass for a small group, and give a little homily. Somewhere in February or March I got out the camera and took a few pictures outdoors, appropriately enough of little flowers like winter aconite and snowdrops and coltsfoot pushing up through the dead leaves of winter or even through the snow.

About the same time I could cope with essential letters that had come in. My handwriting was pretty shaky: the pills I take make controlling a pen difficult at the best of times. Now and then I typed a letter to make it look better. Soon I could face the task of answering ordinary letters without making the recipients as depressed as I was myself. Doing duty at the reception desk when my turn came around was the next hurdle. Then I began to take the good advice of going for at least a short walk every day: being still a free agent I was able to choose the time that gave me the most benefit from the walk, after breakfast.

Library books have been a great help in all my periods of recovery, and about this time I began to be able to concentrate well enough to get through a whole book, and I had enough mental energy to go to the village library for a change of books. Probably somewhere in March I began to look ahead at my diary to see what retreats and other work I had engaged to do when the house programme was made out. Some of the work I had had to abandon while ill, and others of the community took up my load for me. I began to prepare for a retreat I had promised to preach in May, and I had to start from scratch as it seemed. My mind seemed to have gone almost blank, until I got started; and then, as the doctor had told me would happen, I found that more and more of the treasures in my mind reappeared out of the mist.

My sickness is an over-excitement followed by a thump down into depression; then comes a slow climb back to a healthy level. *Manic-depressive* is, I believe, the proper description of the sequence. There is a turning point in the depression, where the main feeling of down, down, down begins to look upwards again. From a depth I begin to look upwards again. There is still a long way to go, back to normal; but I am no longer getting more and more depressed. So for a couple of months after the worst of the illness, each time I find the depression goes on without my feeling any better, but rather worse: I gradually come to myself and remember in the cold light of day all the embarrassing things I did and said and wrote in the illness; my mind seems like a blank, my skills seem gone and my life in ruins. Then comes this day after a couple of months or so, when life seems at last to take a turn for the better. From now on, the graph turns upwards, in spite of many tears still to shed.

Next on the list came driving a car again. Whilst ill I could not possibly have driven in safety; then it seemed I would never drive again – till one day I suddenly know I can do it again. In a house like ours, there is often someone who needs to be driven to the railway station or collected from a train, and for me at this stage driving is a way of helping the daily work of the community without having to preach or face a group of people. Soon afterwards I began to hear confessions of people coming on retreat, and to say Mass and preach the homily for the larger groups of laypeople who come to us. After a while, when one of the other priests of the community was sick and confined to bed, I found I could cope with finding out what he could manage for his meals and bringing it to him — a little thing, but it saved anyone else who was busier having to see to the invalid.

All through these months I was completely supported by the community of Jesuits and Loreto Sisters who work on the team here, along with the new Superior we have had since September 1985. They never complain that I am not pulling my weight, they never rush me or expect me to do any of the work of the house before I know myself to be ready.

When I went to the doctor again in April, I was relieved to hear him say that I should not give up writing just because writing and the sickness had more than once got mixed up with one another. To be able to write is a gift from God, he said, and he reminded me I had written three books, edited four others and devised three sets of school workcards, all without getting ill. All sorts of areas of my life got mixed up with the illness, not just my writing. So now I feel encouraged to be writing the last chapter of this story of mine, so long as I am not getting unduly wrapped up in the telling of the tale. Another thing he said which encouraged me greatly: the longer and slower the recovery from depression, the gentler the gradient of the rise back to normal, the more likely I shall be to stay at a healthy level once I reach a healthy level. A sudden recovery can escalate above a healthy level into over-excitement all over again, but a slow recovery stands a better chance of long-term success. This is consoling information to one who wonders will he ever get better, because recovery is taking so long.

My doctor has often suggested that I write up these stages of recovery from depression, especially as they are seen from a religious point of view. That is what I am trying to do in these pages, here and in the illustrations from Scripture which follow. But I did not feel able to write about my recovery without telling the story of my getting ill in the first place, which really called for a summary of my life before that.

In May I was able to preach the retreat for thirty or so older Sisters, giving a couple of talks a day and being available for interviews and confessions. One of the others of the community most kindly acted as support, in case I should ever feel unable to carry on, and helped with all the practicalities and all the services. The next big hurdle ahead will be in July, when I am on the programme to be one of the directors for a 'directed retreat', that is to say a one-to-one retreat where there are no formal talks to the group of retreatants, but each one is dealt with separately and privately. I have started preparation, because at first my mind was almost a complete blank, in spite of my having directed retreatants many times in the past. So I am building up again my own collections of favourite Scripture passages and guidelines for spiritual direction.

Other things I have taken up are to finish this last section of my 'Journey', to assemble material for an autumn retreat which will have a topic I have never given retreats on before, and to start collecting material for another book I would like to write when this one is finished. Being now able to face a long, calm, look at my notes collected over the years, I find that the drastic pruning I have tended to do while ill has done less damage than I feared. The blanks in my mind continue to fill in with meaning as I go over the notes and rediscover old treasures.

Before too long I will hope to be able to face going out and about to visit those of my old friends who are within reach. I do not know why I cannot cope with friends until I am firmly back on an even keel again, but there it is — I must heal first. Each Christmas and Easter brings many, many cards and letters from old friends and from relations, so I know they are still out there. No doubt my blindness or paralysis with regard to dear friends will dissolve and fade away, and I will wonder how I ever doubted their love and understanding. Really the reason for my sudden shyness is the deep conviction that I must get better here at home before venturing out into the wider world I used to inhabit until four years ago.

Hill-climbers coming down the far side of the hill can still have their falls through over-eagerness. I will always remember tripping up as I came down the Sugar Loaf mountain in Dublin carrying a small boy on my shoulders. He had further to fall than I did, but mercifully he was all in one piece and less shaken than I was. Likewise in the story of my life I do not expect to be free of all troubles just because I am on the way downhill towards home.

One feature of my life I do not expect ever to go back to is playing the guitar to accompany myself singing. For twenty-one years, from 1960 to 1981, this was my chief hobby: I learnt over three hundred songs as the years went by, and played and sang at hundreds of concerts and sing-songs. When the time came for leaving Liverpool city in 1981, I gratefully put the guitar away and decided to join the audience from now on. Maybe for a professional singer it is different, but I found that in the last year I was growing heartily tired of the old favourites everyone kept requesting, and yet more and more stretched to keep learning new songs. It was only a hobby, so I dropped it and took up an interest in wild flowers instead. But I shall always be grateful to my guitar, which helped me to sing so many songs and led me to so many friends I would never otherwise have met. Now that I am a retired guitarist, I find if I listen to the right radio station that never a day goes by without their playing one of my three hundred songs (I chose perennial favourites wherever possible). I recall how in my playing days often one or another of my regular listeners would tell me, 'I heard one of your songs on the radio'. These days it is pleasant to think that my old listeners may still be recognizing 'my' songs on the radio and remembering happy times. Mentioning the radio reminds me to record how grateful I have been for the company it provides without ever intruding, especially in the early days of recovery when I cannot concentrate well enough to read.

One more item of interest to me, which may have something to do with having reached the top of the mountain and started down the other side, is that only in the past year have I started to tell people, in talks to retreatants, about the dream I had while in a coma, as I have written it above. For twenty-five years I had kept it a complete secret. Perhaps now that I am on the way down and within sight of home, the question of whether I should hug it to myself, for want of clear instructions to do otherwise, or see if listeners liked to hear it, no longer seemed to matter. So now I tell it, when the moment seems right.

This seems a good moment, here at the final instalment of my story to date, to tell of one of my earliest memories of childhood. We three children had all caught whooping-cough, an affliction probably even more serious then than now. When I was well enough to get up, I discovered to my dismay that I had forgotten how to walk. Nothing could induce me to get up and go. Then someone had the bright idea of getting out from storage the leather harness and reins with which we had all three been encouraged in our early steps as toddlers. I can remember being set up for the great experiment in the front hall of our house. I was dressed up in my blue outdoor coat, the harness was put on; either our mother or our father gathered up the reins behind me; I was propped up on my feet, set my sights on the front door there at the end of the hall, and away I walked. My brother and sister sent up a cheer, because the reins were being held so lightly behind me that I was in fact walking again.

3·'ENOUGH FOR ME TO KEEP MY SOUL TRANQUIL'

Such is the story of my life up to the present, perhaps not the cheeriest of finishes to a story, but every story can be transformed and transfigured by the light of Scripture. The Bible can make sense of what must otherwise seem senseless. The first passage of the gospels which came to my aid as I came to myself again after the last illness was the story of Gethsemane (Mark 14:32–42). I would pick up a rosary and hold it at the 'first sorrowful mystery', unable to say a word but somehow knowing I was in the right place: 'Abba! (Father!). . .Take this cup away from me.'

Jonah was a help too, in the early days of recovery. If Jonah could still be safe in the hands of God after running away from God's will as fast as his legs and a boat could carry him, then there was hope for me. There is a certain fellow-feeling for Jonah, since coming back to normal after mental illness feels not unlike being vomited up on the seashore by a whale (cf. Jonah 2:11). After such a rocky ride one needs time to dry out and to wonder where to go next.

I was so clearly unable to achieve any of the normal activities of a priest while ill and in the early months of recovery, that it was obvious I must rely on nothing but God's promises for my salvation. In my heart I knew this: we are sons and daughters of God, able to call him 'my Father!', and if sons and daughters then heirs also. Heaven is our inheritance (cf. Galatians 4:6f.). But at the same time no one likes being useless or feeling useless and being completely unable to do anything about the situation. Yet underneath all the sorrow and dismay, peace is still there, not as the world knows peace but the kind that can co-exist with pain and tears (cf. John 14:27).

Not for the first time in my life I treasured the thought that Jesus my good shepherd is not sitting sulking where I should have been, but is here with me, not asking whose fault the illness is nor why I am where I am. One of the photographs I took last year I took because the subject reminded me of the figure and attitude of Jesus as I saw him in my coma dream. For the same reason I have it among the pictures on the wall of my room, where without a word

I can look at it and remember the good shepherd. In the early days of recovery I would wish many times that the shepherd would pick me up and carry me home (cf. Luke 15:5). His answer seems to be, that the day for carrying me home will come, but not yet. In the meantime, the very fact that my shepherd asks no questions lightens my heart, and makes me no longer a burden to myself.

A dear friend of mine who has suffered a lot from depression said to me, very truly, that learning to do things again after depression is like painfully learning to walk as a child all over again, never being sure the earth will be there underfoot for the next step. Several Scripture images express the same sensation. Peter walking on the waves is one of them (cf. Matthew 14:28–33): for Peter it was seemingly not enough that he had taken one step or two steps, he still did not know that his next step had any guarantee of success, enough to make him go forward confidently. A similar story with, for me, a similar message is that of Elijah and the widow of Zarephath (cf. 1 Kings 17:7–16). Each day was an act of faith: use up the little flour and the little oil which seems to be all there is left, and trust there will be more tomorrow. 'I believe for today; help the little faith I have so that I may count on tomorrow as well.'

When it came to preparing sermons and talks all over again, as one who had forgotten how it was done and what to say, the story of the five loaves and the two fishes encouraged me (cf. Mark 6:30–44). Jesus is saying 'Give the people something to eat yourself', and in my empty head and heart there seems not to be enough to give so many people something to eat. But then I start with the little I have, and it turns out to be enough and something over.

If the top of my life's mountain was the last stay in hospital, that time in Liverpool, then I repeat that I for one have no desire to remain at the summit, nor any wish to go back there. To continue the metaphor, the ground under me there at the top was hard and sharp as rock, visibility was nil, the wind was piercing. There were ministering angels, in the shape of the doctors and nurses and chaplains. In an obscure way I was aware at that time that 'Yahweh is my rock' (cf. Psalm 18:2), but the experience was too much for me. Like Elijah on the mountain (or so it seemed to me), I was relieved when the mighty wind gave place to the earthquake, the earthquake to the fire and the fire to the gentle breeze, the 'still, small voice', as I left hospital and began to get better (cf. 1 Kings 19:9–18). The small voice was saying even then that I was over the worst and need not climb any further.

As for not being jealous of those who seem to have had an easier time of it, a ride to the top of their own mountain, the last word must surely be that which Jesus puts on the lips of the owner of the vineyard when the labourers complain of his seeming bias towards the latecomers: 'Have I no right to do what I like with my own? Why be envious because I am generous?' (cf. Matthew 20:15). We must be compassionate as our Father is compassionate (cf. Luke 6:36).

I do not know of any Scripture passage that would compare the latter part of our lives to the far side of our own mountain, as we go down at a different pace from the ascent. How I, for my own prayers, fit the picture in with a favourite passage of Scripture is like this: I go back to the story of the prodigal son, the father and the elder brother (cf. Luke 15:11–32). I, the lost son, reappear over the top of the mountain and the Father sees me coming, a long way off. Moved with pity, he runs up the hill to meet me, and together we walk back down the hill towards home, where Jesus is preparing the supper ('the supper of the Lamb', cf. Revelation 19:9). There we will see Jesus, as he told us (cf. Mark 16:7). 'Home' is heaven, in this way of looking at the story, which means that our Father comes running to meet his lost children long before we die, while we are still a long way from dying, and the last part of the journey is travelled together, Father and child. Jesus is then like the elder brother (Friend and Brother, as St Richard of Chichester calls him), only completely at one with our Father, willing to share his Father's love and his own inheritance with us, preparing for the arrival of his brothers and sisters with a warm welcome and a feast.

Jesus at the Last Supper told us,

> If anyone loves me he will keep my word,
> and my Father will love him,
> and we shall come to him
> and make our home with him. (John 14:23)

Since both Father and Son will come to dwell with us as we journey home, perhaps we are justified in picturing life either as a journey with the Son towards the Father, or with the Father towards the Son. In either case it is possible to 'walk humbly with our God':

> This is what Yahweh asks of you:
> only this, to act justly,
> to love tenderly
> and to walk humbly with your God. (Micah 6:8)

For the first twenty-four years of my life I tried to act justly, then found the task beyond me and had to leave it to Jesus to justify me. Then for the next twenty-four years I tried to love tenderly, only to find I could not keep that up on my own, either. So I had to leave it to Jesus to gather his own and my lambs and sheep. Now walking downhill with my God, less ambitious than before, I hope to manage this stage for a while until at last I can go no further: then the Shepherd will carry me the rest of the way.

Psalm 131 is called a Song of Ascents. I love it now more deeply than ever before, and think it could rather be called a Song of Descent:

> Yahweh, my heart has no lofty ambitions,
>   my eyes do not look too high.
> I am not concerned with great affairs
>   or marvels beyond my scope.
> Enough for me to keep my soul tranquil and quiet
>   like a child in its mother's arms,
> as content as a child that has been weaned.
>
> Israel, rely on Yahweh,
>   now and for always! (Psalm 131)

As we walk home, whether with the Son towards the Father, or with the Father towards the Son, we are going towards our inheritance. 'I gave you a land where you never toiled, you live in towns you never built; you eat now from vineyards and olivegroves you never planted' (Joshua 24:13). Our inheritance will be better than any reward we could have toiled for.

St Luke the physician tells us of the time Jesus called out the spirit of an unclean devil from a man, and the devil, throwing the man down in front of everyone, went out of him 'without hurting him at all' (cf. Luke 4:33–37). This always suggests to me that however much the evil spirit may have distressed the man in the past, now the man is as good as new, as if he had never been afflicted. Jesus in his resurrection is apparently in a similar condition: not that he was unhurt in his sufferings, Heaven knows, but now in his resurrection he is beyond being hurt in time or eternity ever again (cf. 1 Corinthians 15:42ff.). His hurts are all healed, and he hardly seems to consider his sufferings worth remembering. 'What things?', he asks the disciples walking to Emmaus, when they marvel at his seemingly not knowing the things that had been happening in Jerusalem in the past few days (cf. Luke 24:19). In the case of gradual healing from my own recurring sickness, I always marvel when one by one my skills come back after I had thought they were gone for ever. The experience helps me to believe in the power of God to keep hidden all that was most precious to me in myself, through sickness and even through death, to give it all back in wholeness and glory. The way in which my skills come back one by one, from deadness to life, from blindness to vision in an almost predictable order, calls to my mind the vision of Ezekiel in the valley of dry bones. He saw what could not be drier or more dead coming together, bone connecting to bone, and the whole coming to full flesh and life anew (cf. Ezekiel 37:1–14).

There is a favourite story of mine in the Old Testament, about Abraham sending the eldest servant of his household, the steward of all his property, to find a bride for his son Isaac from among Abraham's people who had not come as far as the Promised Land (cf. Genesis 24). This was a very responsible mission, but to take the strain out of the task, Abraham made quite clear to his servant that if the right girl, once found, would not come back with him, then he would be free of all obligation in the matter. This story strikes me as being a good illustration of what I mean by walking downnhill with God rather than, as formerly, climbing uphill towards him. The task is no longer all-important. The servant simply does his best and then returns in peace to his master, whatever the success or failure. Abraham made his burden light for the servant; Jesus makes every burden light for us. At least, Jesus tells us his burden is light (cf. Matthew 11:30), which must mean that if we find ourselves carrying a heavy burden, that burden is not of Jesus. We should drop it if we can.

Moses on the way through the wilderness with the people complained to Yahweh: he, Moses, never conceived all these people, so why should he have to carry them in his bosom, like a nurse with a baby at the breast? Yahweh in reply lets Moses choose seventy of the elders to share his burden. If Moses could reach a point where he could no longer cope with his people, no wonder that the rest of us lesser mortals sometimes find our own people more than we can carry any longer. I remember visiting a mother who was dying of cancer: she was not worried about herself, but about her young child whom she was having to leave behind. Not just Jesus the shepherd, but many another shepherd and shepherdess, is stricken, and their sheep scattered (cf. Zechariah 13:7; Mark 14:27). Our life in Christ encourages us in the hope that our sheep and lambs will be gathered round us again in the resurrection (cf. Mark 14:28; 16:7).

When Moses and the people were about to set out from Mount Sinai to make their way through the wilderness towards the Promised Land, Moses wanted a guide, someone like his father-in-law who had lived thereabouts all his life and who knew the territory, to lead them all safe from one oasis to the next. 'Do not leave us', said Moses to Hobab (also named Jethro) his father-in-law, 'for you know where we can camp in the wilderness, and so you will be our eyes. If you come with us, you will share in the blessing of the happiness with which Yahweh blesses us' (cf. Numbers 10:31f.). I hope that my story as I have written it in these pages may help some others to find their way through the wilderness years of their own lives.

4·WE ARE ALL GOING *HOME*

Each part of my journey described so far has contained a final section to help readers find their own lives pictured there, like mine, under the light of Scripture. I hope that this seventh part of the story may have helped others who suffer from depression, to believe that all the things they held dear are not lost, but are being kept for them by their heavenly Father, until they are ready to receive them again. The story of Jesus' resurrection helps us to believe that not only will the ill-effects of depression be reversed, but also the results of physical sickness or surgery or advancing years.

For myself, I find very helpful the picture of life as a climb up a mountain followed by a climb down the other side towards home, and I think I can see the same pattern reflected in the lives of many others. People who have retired from work, for instance, would surely be glad to know they are not expected by God to climb any more mountains, since their mountain is already climbed. Now they go, ever more gently, towards home where Jesus their Friend and Brother is preparing a welcome. I am convinced the change from uphill to downhill happens to many others while they are still at work, as it did to me. The day comes when they are no longer driven by ambition, either for themselves or in the service of God; they come to realize that life could go by in striving for impossible goals, and they leave off the race to go ever higher. Instead they begin to relax more and enjoy what they have. Either that or they turn cynical, secretly sad over their highest ambitions not achieved — such a pity, since our Father only invites us to scale our own mountain and then walk contentedly with him down the other side.

When we start out on our journey in search of God, we find Jesus offering to lead us along the way; so he leads and we follow. At some stage, he goes ahead faster than we can follow, and we think we have lost him. But then we find he is within us, looking out through our own eyes: we feel we can say with St Paul, 'I live now not with my own life but with the life of Christ who lives in me' (Galatians 2:20). Then we hear Jesus saying as at the Last Supper: 'I am in the Father and the Father is in me' (John 14:11), so those who are in Jesus must be in the Father and the Father in them. The journey into God, for me at any rate, has seemed like a following of Jesus, then a closer union with Jesus, then a closer union with the Father; and I know that the journey for many, many others follows the same road. Now through Jesus, and with him, and in him we offer our eyes, our hands, our hearts, our all to the Father who is within us.

I would hope that the many who are out of work through no wish of their own will still be able to recognize features of their own lives within the seven stages of my life pictured in these pages. Those who are at an age where they are now unlikely to find paid work again must sooner or later come to terms with their situation, and understand that God is a loving Father who does not ask the impossible. For Jesus, 'work' means 'working for God', and 'This is working for God: you must believe in the one he has sent' (cf. John 6:29). Jesus, the one our Father sent, is the one whose burden is light. The Letter to the Hebrews has encouraging words for those who feel they have not done enough to deserve to be walking downhill home, and that it is now too late: 'None of you must think that he has come too late for the . . . place of rest' (cf. Hebrews 4:1).

Equally encouraging is the true thought that we are all going *home*, and not to a strange land. The Father chose each of us in Christ his Son before the world was made; he sent each of us into the world to do his work and called us back to himself in Christ, so we are going home. Many poets and writers have illustrated the journey of life as a journey home, from Homer in the *Odyssey* to G. K. Chesterton in his short story *The Coloured Lands*. Chesterton depicts a little boy dissatisfied with the view at home, who is given free access to travel through a green land, a blue land, a red land, a yellow land and all the rest of the coloured lands. Then he is given a brush and large pots of each of the colours, to paint his own view. He paints it confidently, only to find he has painted the view at home he started with. Home is where we started, and home is where we are going, and the Spirit is our homesickness. The story of the Prodigal Son gives us Jesus' authority for expecting a welcome at home from our Father, who will even come to meet us, just as all Jesus' teaching centres on his bringing us to call God our Father. Home is where our Father lives.

Those of us who are sick with an illness that is unlikely to go away, and that includes the failing of some of our powers with advancing years, will find it easier to come to terms with our situation if we understand our Father has already met us and is accompanying us on the rest of the journey. In a sense we are already home, but we are still blind to the beauty of the love that awaits our sight, when we finally see Jesus as he promised us. Archbishop Roberts, the English Jesuit who became Archbishop of Bombay and then returned to a lively retirement in London, once compared life's journey to bringing home a crippled ship. Not just the later years of life but the whole of life is like being captain of a crippled ship, and bringing her home.

We all tend to feel still responsible for those we were once responsible for, and this is good and true. Parents and teachers and priests, doctors and nurses, youth leaders, friends, all these and many other kinds of people are shepherds, and good shepherds do not desert their flocks. But there is a vital difference between having a shepherd's love for our lambs and sheep, and *feeling guilty* because they have not turned out as we hoped, or because we have lost touch with them. Better far to accept the loss of these loved ones as the 'striking of the shepherd', beyond which will come the gathering of the flock into one again. Our sorrow is for their healing. In the case of parents, especially, Jesus would want us to do as the elder brother of the prodigal was asked to do, and keep a welcome for the lost ones always. Heaven would be flawed for us without those we have loved; if we can forgive them, certainly their Father has forgiven them already.

We must extend our love and forgiveness, too, to all those our Father loves and has forgiven, whoever they may be. Once we have arrived at our heavenly home, we will be expected to welcome all our enemies as we ourselves were welcomed by our Father. So the closer we are to our homecoming, the more we must get into the way of praying for those who have ever hurt us, and for those we are tempted to think do not deserve to share heaven with us. As we begin to look at the world with our Father's eyes, we must be prepared to welcome all his children, wherever they may be. The martyr St Edmund Campion wrote a letter to Queen Elizabeth I, who was head of the government persecuting him and in his eyes a heretic, looking forward to their meeting as friends at last in heaven, 'when all injuries shall be forgotten'. In imitation of Jesus on the cross, and like so many saints and martyrs, the closer we come to our journey's end the more we must pray for our enemies, so that 'we may at last be friends in heaven'.

Loyola Hall
13 June 1986

Epilogue

KEEPING ON COURSE AND LOOKING FORWARD TO THE KINGDOM

A year and a quarter has gone by since the story of my journey was written. How is the journey going on now? Certainly I am a lot more cheerful and a little more confident than a year ago. Maybe I shall never fully regain my old confidence, but I am still travelling, and the journey is still worth while. In one respect there has been a big step forward: I can now recognize for myself when my mood is getting high and over-excited. More than once I have been able to damp down various activities like creative writing or photography for the time being, because they were starting to make my head spin. The psychiatrist seems to be both surprised and pleased about this, because usually patients are the last people to see that they are getting too elated.

This clearer sight of myself started about a year ago. I began to take careful note of the signs in myself that tell me I am depressed, and the different signs that tell me I am 'high'. It also struck me then that there are two ways of reacting to my moods. Either I can go along with them and reinforce them, or I can go in the other direction and bring them under control. Thus when I am depressed, the thing to do to make life more bearable is to keep very busy and choose plenty of company. When I am over-excited on the other hand, too much busy-ness and company just makes me worse excited, so the thing to do is to go easy and keep myself to myself more. But unless I know for certain whether I am 'high' or 'low' on any given day, I could unknowingly be making a depression worse or making a mood of excitement into something dangerous. This kind of plan of action, working against the prevailing mood, is not enough by itself to effect a cure, but it does me good to feel I am supporting the work of the medicines and not simply cancelling them out. It is clearly invaluable to know when it is time to take one of the tablets that damp down over-excitement, *before* I go out of control, rather

111

than to have somebody else give me a lot of the same tablets in hospital because I already went out of control.

Another great blessing over the past two years has been the fact that the Superior of the house here is a trained and qualified counsellor. Very frequently to begin with, and nowadays about once a fortnight, I am able to tell him exactly what has been happening, all my feelings and reactions good, bad and indifferent, and to share any anxieties. At the heart of his special skills is that of listening; and then when the time is right he feeds back to me significant things I have said in the past. I make a list as the days go by of the things I want to talk about, and when the list itself starts to be a burden we have a session. All of this acts as a mirror in which to understand, and therefore cope with, my daily life. My meetings every few months with the psychiatrist are all the easier and more helpful for having had the conversations at home with the Superior in the meantime.

I still feel happy and comfortable in the imagined framework of the climb up the Mediterranean Steps. That is to say, I still feel happy and comfortable to be walking quietly down the gentler side of the Rock in the company of my Father. I still feel happy that Jesus has gone on ahead to prepare the supper for when we reach home. No need to go into this again or to point out the basis in Scripture for such a way of thinking and imagining. I am conscious that the Father leaves it to me, when we come to a crossroads, to choose which way to go. He must be leaving it to the homing instinct within me, to adjust if I go too far to one side to the other.

Sometimes I like to think of the same reality under a different guise. I imagine that I am in my boat, steering. Jesus is in my boat, asleep with his head on the helmsman's cushion, as he was in Peter's boat. When the going gets rough, I have to stand up anyway to cope with the tiller, and I don't need the cushion. My aim is to keep a straight course. My shifting moods, like the winds and the tides, keep trying to push me off course; so all the time I must lean against them, first one way and then the other, to keep the boat going in a straight line. To keep the picture uniform with the other picture of walking down the hill, I think to myself that Jesus is perhaps not in the boat at all but on the further shore ready to help pull the boat in when we get there; the Father is with me in the boat, saying nothing but letting me learn the art of steering.

My key motto now as always is 'Behold, your servant am I, ready for anything'. Today serving God seems to mean for me first and foremost this constant work of steering: to watch my mood, to go hard against depression, to go easy if high. If in doubt as to whether I am high or low, I treat it as high for safety's sake. Surely if I keep on leaning, like a steersman, against the prevailing swing, then I shall keep on course and be able to do the daily tasks that God asks of me. Major decisions may be taken in safety only if I am neither too high nor too low, so my main task for God is to try and keep balanced somewhere in the middle.

And what about being 'ready for anything', now, when so often I have to ask not to be given this or that task, because I am not ready for it yet? When I was young I took this part of my motto to mean, as expressed in the Jesuit Constitutions, 'ready to be sent anywhere in the world to attempt any job in the world'. Nowadays, after so many trips to hospital, and so much later in life, the options are clearly fewer — so how do I interpret this being 'ready for anything'? I am ready to go back into hospital or to stay well, *and still believe in God's love for me;* I am ready to take the disappointment of not being able to fulfil lifelong ambitions, *and still believe God loves me;* I am ready if the unexpected happens, good or bad, *still to believe in God's closeness.*

On the subject of God's closeness, it seemed to me at first as if the Father had greeted me his prodigal somewhere along the road and then walked beside me down towards home and Jesus. But pretty soon it seemed to be truer to say that God is in my eyes, seeing what I see, in my ears, hearing what I hear, in my heart and mind, feeling and understanding what I feel and think. We all of us have an inner sanctuary where God belongs to us and nobody else, a place where each of us is the one closest to his heart. He is our parent and a good parent loves each of the children one by one even before he loves them all together as a family. This is now the last stage of the journey, and God is to each of us what he was in the beginning – but there has been a mountain climbed in the meantime, thanks to Jesus.

The gospel story in St Luke of the rich man and Lazarus helps me still, especially when duty calls me to the various works of the retreat house I live in. Certainly after all this training and experience I have riches to spare, and it is good, in the nervous hours before a new retreat begins, to recall Jesus' insistence that we share our riches. The traffic is not all one way: colleagues and guests alike are at least as generous in sharing their riches with the Lazarus that is in me. There is something specially appealing in the picture of Lazarus, begging, covered with sores, comforted by the house-dogs even if by nobody else. Rather than be afraid of the strangers who come to our door as guests, I remind myself that they each have, as I have, sores to be healed and a hunger to be filled.

One final Scripture message I try never to forget is that about forgiving others as we hope to be forgiven ourselves. I still from time to time go down the list of any and all who may have hurt me in my lifetime, and pray for them all, by name if I remember their names. I pray too for the many people I must have hurt in my life; if they see me as an enemy for what I did to them, then I pray for them.

My work-load these days is still a good deal lighter than anyone else's in the house. As my confidence increases and I begin to take the various tasks more calmly, so I can do a little more. On the other hand any social life outside the community is still very restricted: not that anyone tells me to stay at home, but my visits out to see old friends simply upset me so much that I cannot cope with them yet, except at wide intervals of time. Writing letters, too, is a thing I cannot bring myself to do when I am at all over-excited; and since I now seem to be somewhat over-excited on at least half the days of my life, that means a lot of friends have to wait a long time for replies to their letters. But then I remember what Jesus said about the shepherd being stricken and the flock scattered before he rose again and gathered them to himself again; and then I look forward to greeting all my friends, relations and benefactors in the kingdom, at the banquet, if not a good deal sooner.

Loyola Hall
8 September 1987

1997 – Ten Years On

Thanks be to God, I am still well and have not been anywhere near hospitals except for a regular check-up. During the whole ten years since the first edition of the book was written I have been a full-time member of the retreat team here at Loyola Hall, taking the same work-load as anybody else on the team. My family are all well and reasonably happy, except for my generous sister Eileen who has recurring back trouble against which she fights to keep active as ever. The two nephews and niece all married, and I now have three lovely great-nieces and a gorgeous baby grand-nephew to date. The Jesuit community and the Sisters and lay retreat staff have seen many changes, and only one of the team who were there in 1987 has continued to the present: Fr David Birchall SJ who has been Director for some years and who is also editor of the hugely successful magazine *Jesuits and Friends*.

In spite of all the changes, the daily feeling of the place has continued happy and I have been very contented. To me the fact of our being a mixed religious/lay, women/men team has been a big plus. Besides that, the local people who do the secretarial work, the cooking and cleaning, the garden and the maintenance, have many of them been with Loyola Hall considerably longer than my two-plus-fourteen years, and the loyalty and friendliness of all of them adds a constant bonus to the atmosphere of the house.

Probably the greatest surprise to me over the past ten years has been the way my book-writing has increased and multiplied. For the most part it has been done as a hobby, and only occasionally have weeks been allotted to me with nothing else to do but write. One blissful six months I was given a half-sabbatical, here at Loyola because here was where I had all my sources and references. The joy of waking up month after month of mornings, with a complete blank of a day ahead and no distractions! I am rarely short of ideas.

The sweetest story about the writing came shortly after I finished writing *The Other Side of the Mountain*. I had to try a few publishers before I found one who would take it on. At the same time, I had completely given up on the book on St Mark's gospel which I had been writing and rewriting ever since studying theology in Ireland in 1961. So much so that one day I said in exasperation to God: 'Well, there it is, one book on St Mark which I thought you had inspired me to write and which nobody seems to want. I've had it. You know where it is. If you want it, you can come and get it!' Within a month, Robert Kelly who was acting as an agent for Ruth McCurry at Geoffrey Chapman came to my room to see about the 'mountain' book, and before he went he asked, 'And have you anything else we might be interested in?' All I had to do was pick up the St Mark manuscript and hand it to him. Ruth published that as well, under the title *Praying St Mark's Gospel*. Twenty-eight years from start to finish.

Public interest in the St Mark book was slow to come, but I received a lot of letters as a result of the 'mountain' life story. Mostly they were very touching, from people who had been through the same sort of brain-storms and who were delighted to read from the inside a story so like their own, but with a fairly happy ending. To me, the most memorable letter was the one from a fellow Jesuit, a classmate of mine at school, who said he nearly fell off his chair in surprise at one point while reading the story: the moment when Father Joe Christie had likened Jesuits to God's odd-job men had been the very moment when he too had decided to apply to the Jesuits! Two with one blow.

The next book I wrote was a logical result of writing the life story. For some time I had been keeping not exactly a diary, but a series of notes to do with the ups and downs of moods and what made them worse, what made them better. Much of the wherewithal for the new book was there already in this book you have just read, but it needed clarifying and codifying, with illustrations and diagrams. I wanted to call it 'Making use of moods', but eventually it came out as *Finding the Still Point* (Eagle, Guildford, 1993), with the other as a subtitle. My proudest moment on that one was seeing what Gerard W. Hughes (author of *God of Surprises*) wrote in his reader's comment for the publisher: that this was the best book on discernment of spirits he had ever read. I have it still, in his own handwriting.

Several of my own photographs, and one of David Birchall's, were included in the book about moods, and I had hopes of branching out as an amateur photographer whose pictures got included in spiritual books, but that never came to anything. What has been very consoling is to be included in the contributors to the series of notelets David devised, called the Loyola Collection and featuring photographs of the house and grounds of Loyola Hall. In fact as each card sells in fives or tens of thousands, and each one is enjoyed by at least two people (the sender and the receiver) the cards reach more people than most books do.

The book on moods has not reached a huge audience, but those who have it do find it very useful. I myself read a little bit of it each day of my life, so as not to forget what I have preached to others. Before it was published in 1993 I tried the material out on a very appreciative group of people at 'Living Theology', a summer school currently held at New Hall in Essex each year. Later on I tried out giving courses in dealing with stress at Loyola Hall a couple of times, but had to abandon the idea: one to one I can be helpful to people in stress, but when there is a whole group of them there together they tend to escalate the tension instead of relieving it. In any case, my real desire for the book is that people should see it as a book for anybody, since we all have moods, and they are the stuff of discernment. The way it came to be published, by the way, is that I was beginning to give up hope for it when Joyce Huggett came to assist at one of our own summer courses, and so I dangled it in front of her. I remember the occasion each time I pass the particular bench in the garden where Joyce was sitting when I plucked up courage to ask her.

There have been holidays as well as work, of course. I have not returned to Gibraltar in the past ten years, though my teacher friend from there has visited here a couple of times. I have travelled to Ireland more than once, to try and catch up with friends and relations there, but more gently than before. I still cannot manage the pace of friendships I used to enjoy before the big breakdown. Madeira is another place I have been to, at the invitation of my sister Eileen; and Switzerland, to visit some hospitable O'Mahony cousins in the summer of 1996.

My guitar remains hung up, though not yet completely parted with. Playing and singing is something I enjoy, but I know only too well how it can escalate into a major preoccupation for me. Besides, I am not as young as I was, and I feel at liberty to choose which hobbies I wish to chase these days. Writing books, taking pictures, observing wild flowers. Those will do. I did long ago have hopes of learning to cook well, but that too I have more or less abandoned. Perhaps most Jesuits of my vintage came to doing the cooking too late in life for any but the 'naturals' to take to it. As it is, I can still enjoy a private retreat time at which I do my own cooking just for myself. The Loreto Sisters in Llandudno have some very attractive self-catering flatlets.

My daily prayers are of a very simple nature. Mostly I just try to talk to God instead of talking to myself, following the advice of Brother Lawrence (of *The Practice of the Presence of God* fame). My desire is to remember all the time that only God and I can see the exact picture that appears to my eyes at any given moment. Only God and I know what the world looks like at this moment from where I find myself: what the person on my right looks like, what the person on my left looks like, from here. What the back of my eyelids looks like, when I close my eyes. I do not have to explain to God, though I would have to explain to anyone else. God is inside me, looking out through my eyes and sharing every experience of sight, sound, taste, touch, smell, feelings, with me. And God cannot be carved up, so I have God's complete attention all the time. Would that God had mine. All this is true for anybody, not just for me.

I also have a 'blind beggar's rigmarole' that I say over many times to God, reminding God of the main things I need. I say 'blind' because the rigmarole contains a clause to the effect that if I am asking for all the wrong things, then please may I have something better instead? In the morning my main prayer is a sorting out of the priorities for the day: out of the things that need doing sometime, which of them need or can be done today? I try to decide this with God, and count it as prayer-time.

Another thing I do to pray when I am tired or restless is to remind myself of the big moments of grace in my life. There have been so many happy times with well-loved people. And there are the special moments of vision which I have described in the main part of this book: the vocation to priesthood and to be a Jesuit, the 'interor castle' experience, the 'rich man and Lazarus' experience, the 'Trinity' experience in the Philosopher's Chapel, the coma dream, and the many, many eye-opening connections that came to my mind when I was writing the book on St Mark. I imagine that book will last when all my others have been forgotten, since it was just given to me. It is the source of everything really worth while in my writings.

There was another special moment of grace back in Dublin near the time of my ordination. I was too shy to mention it when doing the 'mountain' book, and besides it is always good to leave out something significant when writing a biography. It creates an air of mystery. What happened was this. I was kneeling praying in my room one day, and behind me on my desk was, closed, the book *The Two-Edged Sword*, by John L. McKenzie SJ. It is an introduction to the Old Testament. On the dust cover is a striking drawing of a shiny Roman two-edged sword against the black background of a cross.

While I was praying, it seemed to me that the sword leapt up off the book and flew around the room near the ceiling, clockwise in front of me and above me. Then it disappeared from my vision, and I thought that was the end of it. But no, it reappeared from the left of me, hilt foremost, and came into my heart, shining most beautifully. Not my heart exactly, since it was exactly half-way, sort of between my lungs. It entered me, slowly, coming to rest, and the doors seemed to close. I have never experienced anything quite like it before or since. There was nothing I could do about it: it happened of its own accord. I even got up to have a look at Fr McKenzie's book, to make sure the sword hadn't disappeared off the dust cover. It hadn't, of course, but that was how real the experience was. I never told anyone about the vision from that day to this, except to one couple who kindly invited me to be best man at their wedding. Afterwards they gave me a present, and it was a paper knife very similar to my memory of the two-edged sword on the dust cover of Fr McKenzie's book. I was so intrigued that they should choose a gift so dear to my heart that I told them what it meant to me. Heaven knows what they made of that.

A tremendous peace and joy came with the vision, and it has been one of the pillars of my existence ever since. Small wonder that I asked during tertianship about becoming a scripture scholar, but in fact the freedom I have had to speak the word of God straight from the heart (or lungs!) has been much more rewarding. Of course the 'two-edged sword' does not apply only to the Old Testament, though it is convenient to think of one edge as what preceded Christ and the other edge as what Jesus brought. For me the 'two-ness' that began to emerge as the years went by related to the two halves of Mark's gospel: the first being all forgiveness and healing, the second being the invitation to take up the cross and follow Jesus.

My next book, which appeared in 1995, was about that: *The Two-Edged Gospel*, it was called. We are saved as lambs, called to be shepherds; we are saved by the light shining on us, we are called to save others by shining the same light on them....and so on and so on, through about fifteen pairs of gospel images. The whole thing is to do with justification by faith, which then calls us to love which can be freely given back to God...or not, and still God will love us.

A few other new thoughts struck me as I was writing *The Two-Edged Gospel*. One of them was that God the First Person is the only One who loves without ever having been loved first: hence the Father's love is totally without strings attached. The Second Person is Love-in-return-for-love. The Holy Spirit is the Relationship, and goes in two directions even in us: faith first, then love. Around this time there was much to-do about not calling God 'He', and I stuck my neck out for still calling God 'He' – with discretion, but with reason also. The reason is that the Second Person of the Trinity and along with that Person every other person in the world is a being capable of being fruitful but unable to be fruitful unless penetrated by the Love-that-was-never-loved-first. But the First Person was never alone, because even that Love cannot be fruitful without a Second Person to accept the love and to love in return. All of which reminds me of the way it is between a man and a woman in marriage and explains why Julian of Norwich writes of God the Father, God the Mother and God the Lord. Not that Jesus was female in any sense, but that his *role* was and is that of a mother...as is our role. There is only one Father, only one original light of love. The rest of us are mirrors.

More recently there have been two other publications, and there is a third in the pipeline. Last winter, I was asked by the Administrator of the Metropolitan Cathedral in Liverpool to write thoughts and prayers to go with a set of photographs of the Way of the Cross in the Cathedral. The sculptor was Sean Rice, and it was a privilege to sit beside him signing the booklet when it appeared. Most sadly, Sean died of a heart attack on the very day the photograph of the occasion appeared in the *Liverpool Echo*. The other recent book is called *Simply Free*, about the freedom of heart that the Good News gives to a Christian (Kevin Mayhew, 1997). The third book will be a book of prayers in the spirit of Ignatius, due to appear in 1998.

Whilst I am recalling unusual happenings I left out of the main part of this life story, here is another that will do nicely as a finale. Back in the noviceship in the winter of 1952/3 I went for a long walk with one of the other novices, Charles Barenbrug. He went to the Vale of Belvoir, not all that far from Harlaxton. There was snow several inches deep, but it was not snowing that day and the roads were clear enough for walking. Quite suddenly there was a sight, a panorama, I will never forget. There were at least eighteen rainbows in the sky at the same time, and two of them were completely circular. The main circular one was about 40° above the horizon all the way round, a complete, huge, rainbow circle. Just above it was another, slightly paler, like an echo of the main one.

In the four corners of the compass there were more rainbows, in the conventional half-circle style. But each of them had an echo rainbow of its own, and also a mirror-image two rainbows, half-circles upside down, above them. I forget what exactly the sun was doing at the time, but the light was beautiful, such as you get towards sunset on a winter's evening in a valley bowl with snow around. So many rainbows, so much colour. My companion didn't seem terribly impressed, and never having heard of such a sight as this I wondered a little if I was 'seeing things'. But if I was, they were very beautiful things. If a rainbow could convince Noah that all was going to be well, then surely eighteen rainbows all at once held lots of promise.

When I began this story I decided to write it in seven stages, because that was the way it happened. In the telling I divided each of the seven stages into four: the Mediterranean Steps image; the straight story; the light the Bible throws on it; the way people live their ordinary lives without so much time for reflection, but still going through the same stages. In my own mind, I was matching each of the seven with succeeding ones of the seven mansions (stopping-off places, inns, suites of rooms) in St Teresa of Avila's classic book *The Interior Castle*. Hence, even writing ten years on, there is no way I can make this an eighth stage: there are only seven. Seven fundamental ways of looking at God, each one getting closer to the truth than the previous one. In my Gibraltar steps image, I am still coming down the other side of the mountain, away from the side when I was climbing all the time. No matter how long it takes, I am still on the way home.